A-Z MIDLANDS

REFERENCE

torway	M54
Under Construction	
Proposed	
torway Junctions with Numbers	
Unlimited Interchange 6 Limited Interchange 8	
torway Service Area (with fuel station)	TROWELL Ⓢ
with access from one carriageway only	Ⓢ
or Road Service Areas (with fuel station)	SHARDLOW
with 24 hour facilities	
nary Route (with junction number)	A50 32
nary Route Destination	NOTTINGHAM
l Carriageways (A & B Roads)	
ss A Road	A513
ss B Road	B5062
or Roads Under Construction	
or Roads Proposed	
l Station	
dient 1:5(20%) & Steeper (Ascent in direction of arrow)	≪
	Toll ▮
eage between Markers	8
way and Station	●
el Crossing and Tunnel	─╫─
er or Canal	
nty or Unitary Authority Boundary	
onal Boundary	─+─+─+
t-up Area	
ige or Hamlet	○
oded Area	
t Height in Feet	• 813
ef Above 400' (122m)	
onal Grid Reference (Kilometres)	¹00
a Covered by Town Plan	SEE PAGE 60

TOURIST INFORMATION

Airport		✈
Airfield		+
Heliport		Ⓗ
Battle Site an...	066	⚔
Castle (open to public)		▉
Castle with Garden (open to public)		▉
Cathedral, Abbey, Church, Friary, Priory		✝
Country Park		Ⓨ
Ferry (vehicular)		⛴ 🚢
(foot only)		▲▲
Garden (open to public)		✿
Golf Course	9 Hole ▶₉	18 Hole ▶₁₈
Historic Building (open to public)		▥
Historic Building with Garden (open to public)		▥
Horse Racecourse		🏇
Lighthouse		⍫
Motor Racing Circuit		🏁
Museum, Art Gallery		▣
National Park		
National Trust Property	(open)	NT
	(restricted opening)	NT
Nature Reserve or Bird Sanctuary		🐦
Nature Trail or Forest Walk		♣
Place of Interest	Monument •	
Picnic Site		⊼
Railway, Steam or Narrow Gauge		🚂
Theme Park		⚓
Tourist Information Centre		ℹ
Viewpoint	(360 degrees)	☀
	(180 degrees)	☀
Visitor Information Centre		Ⓥ
Wildlife Park		⍦
Windmill		𝕏
Zoo or Safari Park		🐘

SCALE

```
0        1        2        3        4        5      6 Miles
0    1    2    3    4    5    6    7    8    9    10 Kilometres
```

Map Pages 4-75
1:158,400
2.5 Miles to 1 Inch

EDITION 1   2024

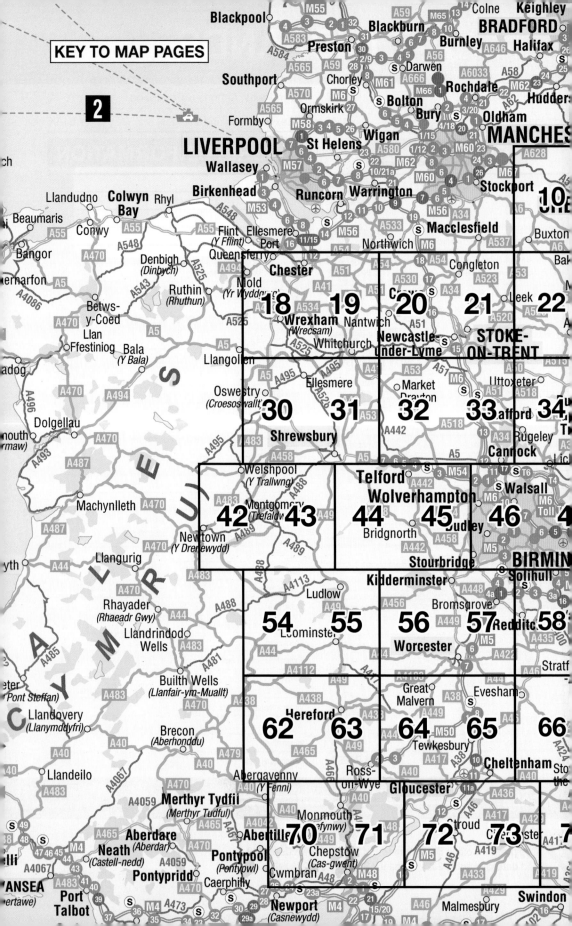

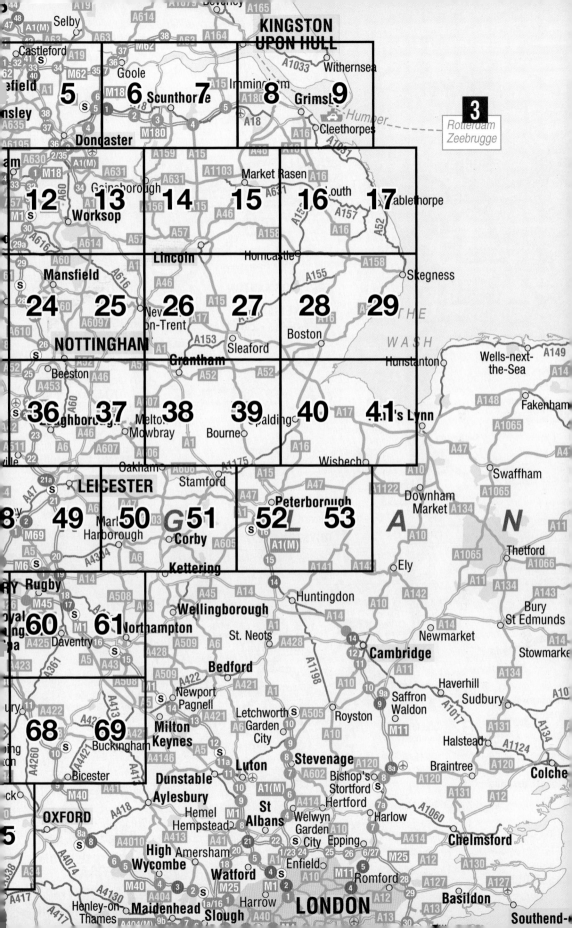

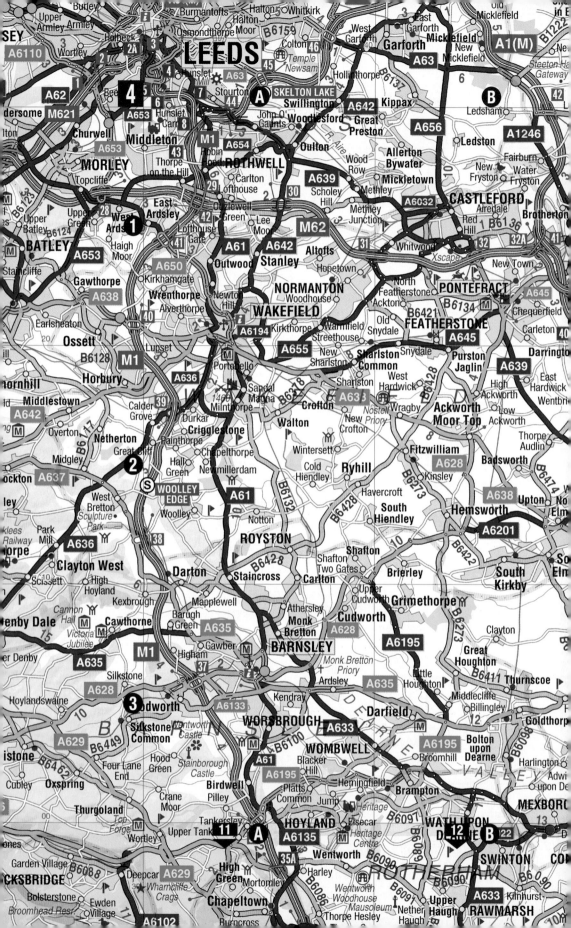

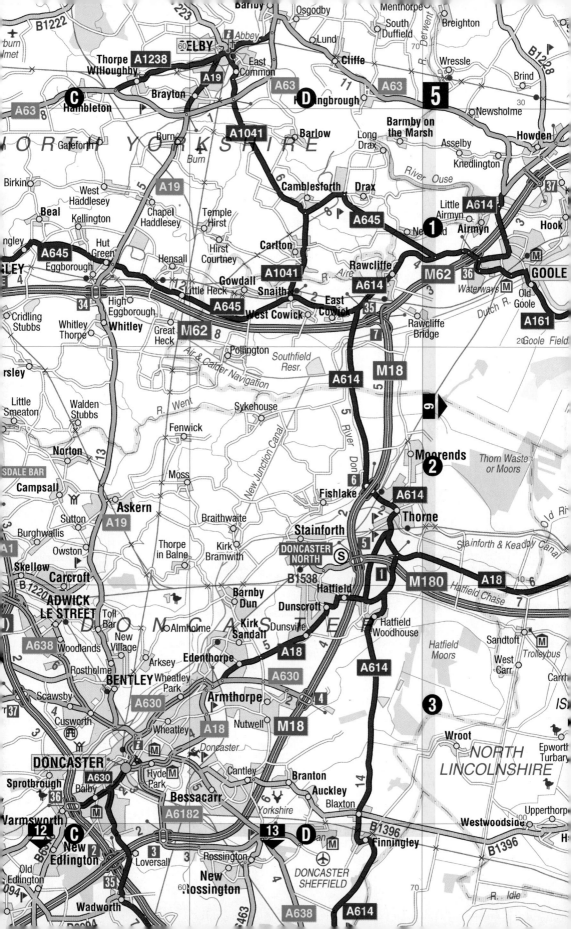

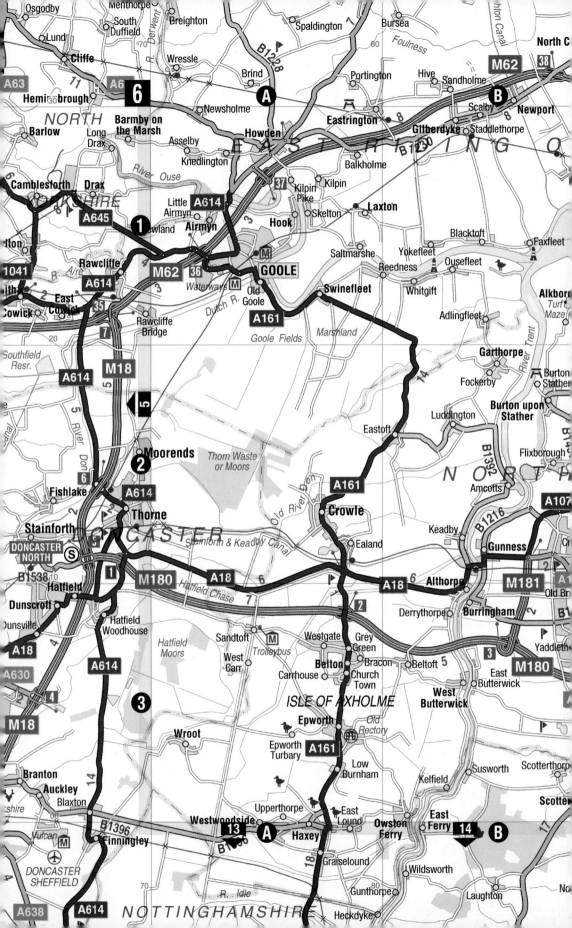

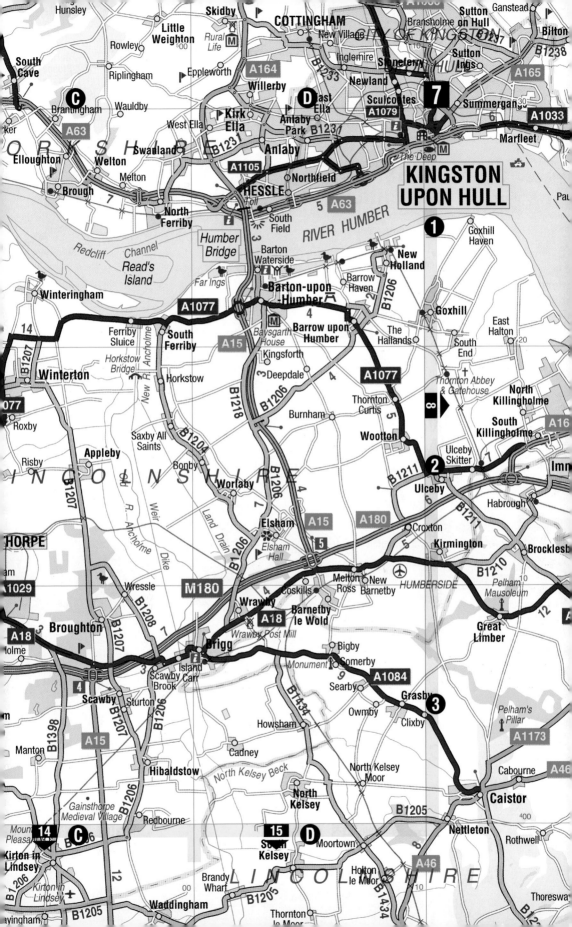

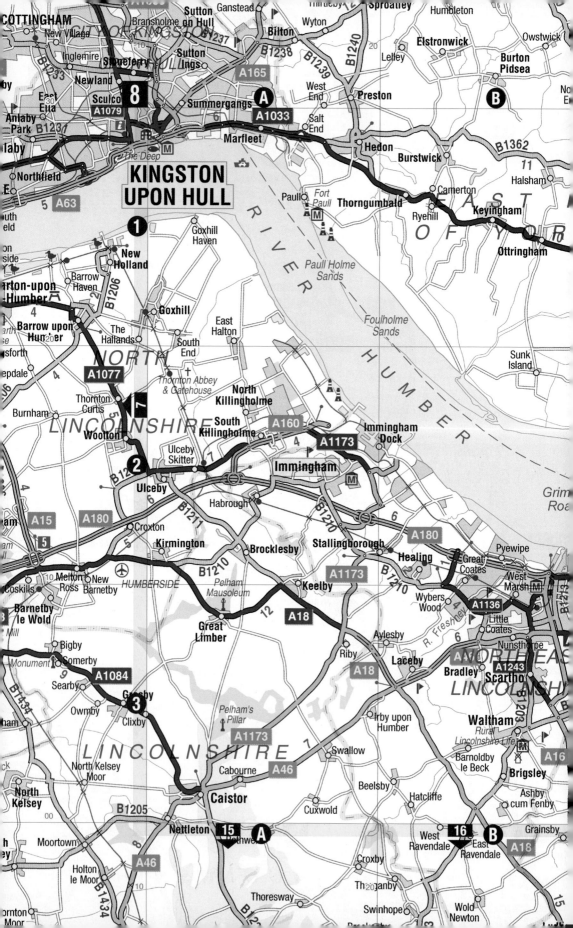

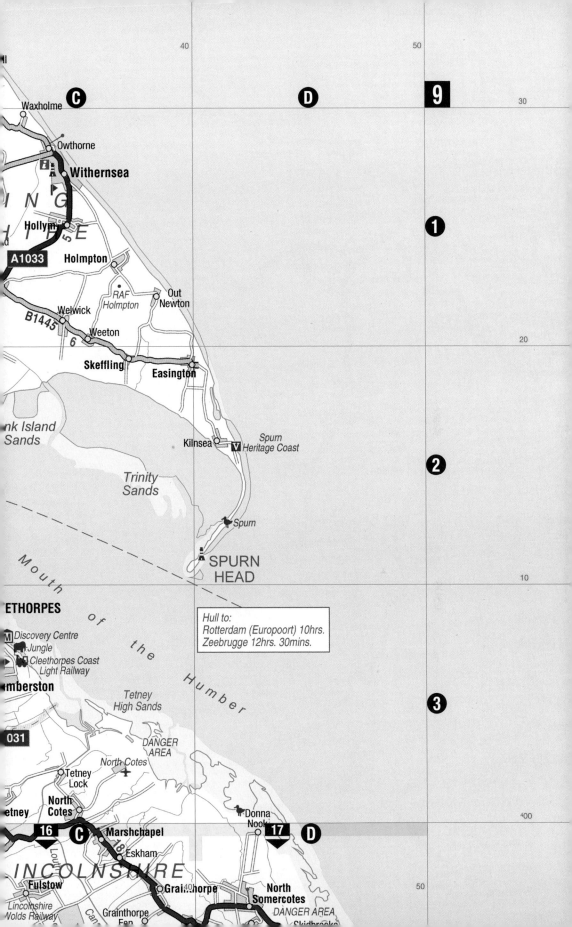

40

50

C

D

9

30

Waxholme

Owthorne

i **Withernsea**

ING

Hollym

1

A1033

Holmpton

RAF
Holmpton

Out
Newton

Welwick

B1445

Weeton

6

Skeffling

Easington

nk Island
Sands

Kilnsea

V Spurn
Heritage Coast

Trinity
Sands

2

Spurn

SPURN
HEAD

Mouth

10

ETHORPES

M Discovery Centre
Jungle
Cleethorpes Coast
Light Railway

of

the

Humber

Hull to:
Rotterdam (Europoort) 10hrs.
Zeebrugge 12hrs. 30mins.

mberston

Tetney
High Sands

3

031

DANGER
AREA

North Cotes

Tetney
Lock

etney

North
Cotes

Donna
Nook

400

16

C

Marshchapel

17

D

Eskham

INCOLNSHIRE

50

Fulstow

Grainthorpe

North
Somercotes

Lincolnshire
Wolds Railway

Grainthorpe
Fen

DANGER AREA

Skidbrooke

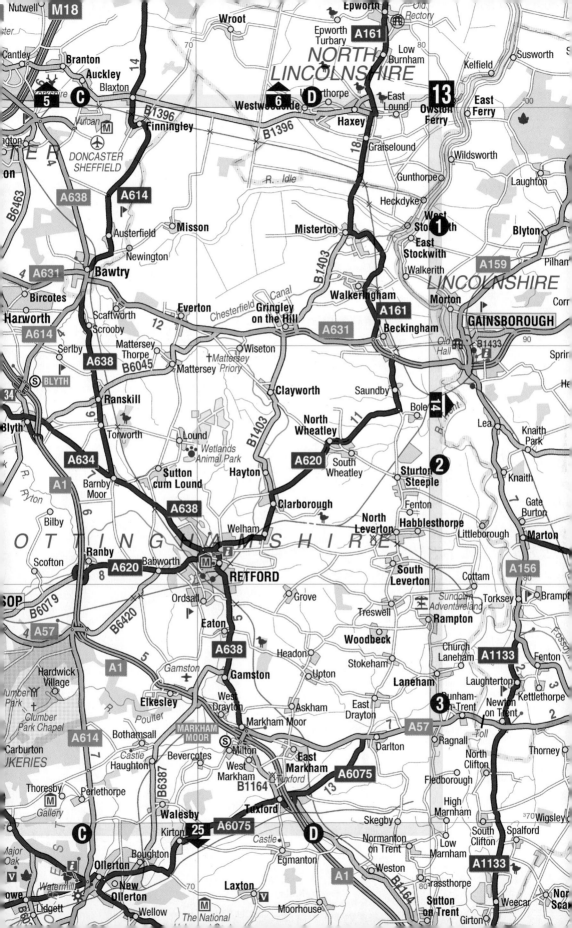

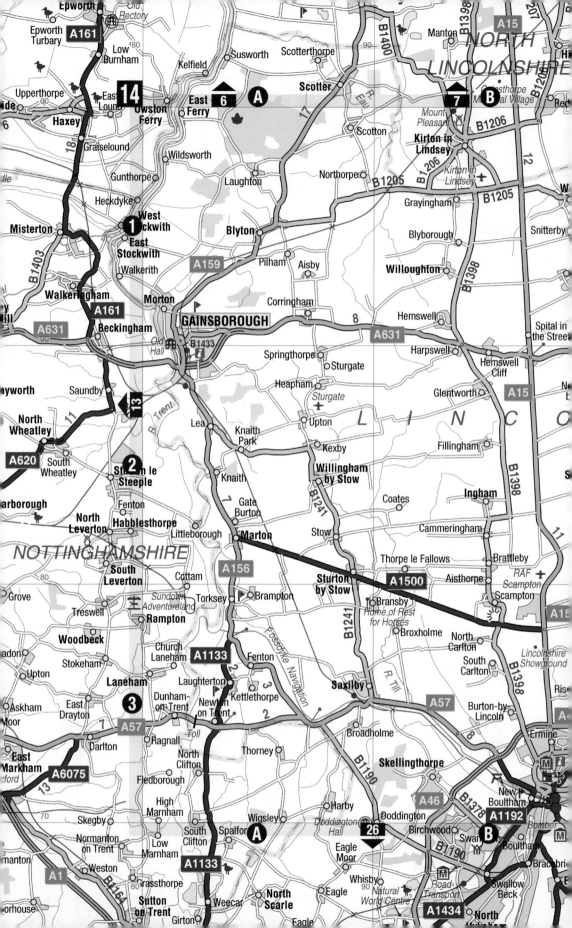

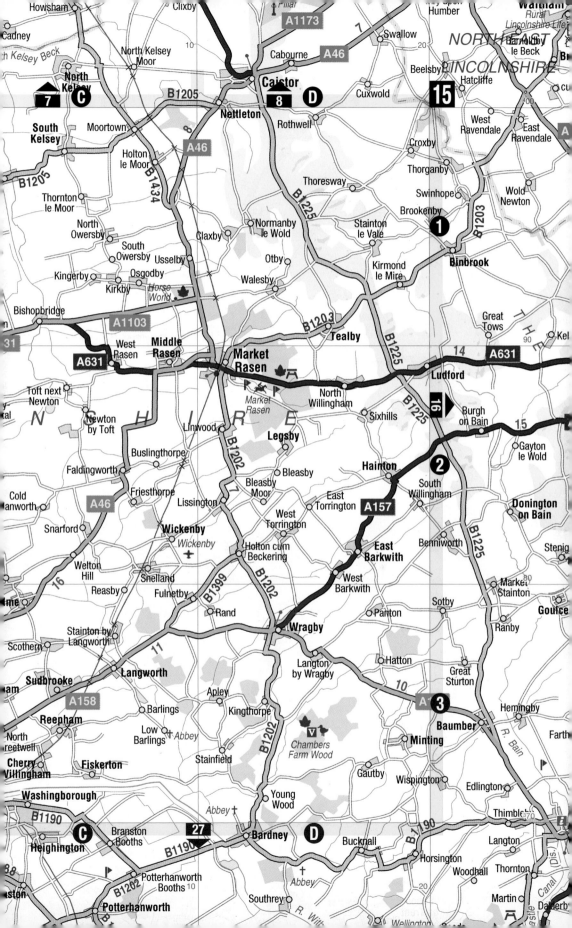

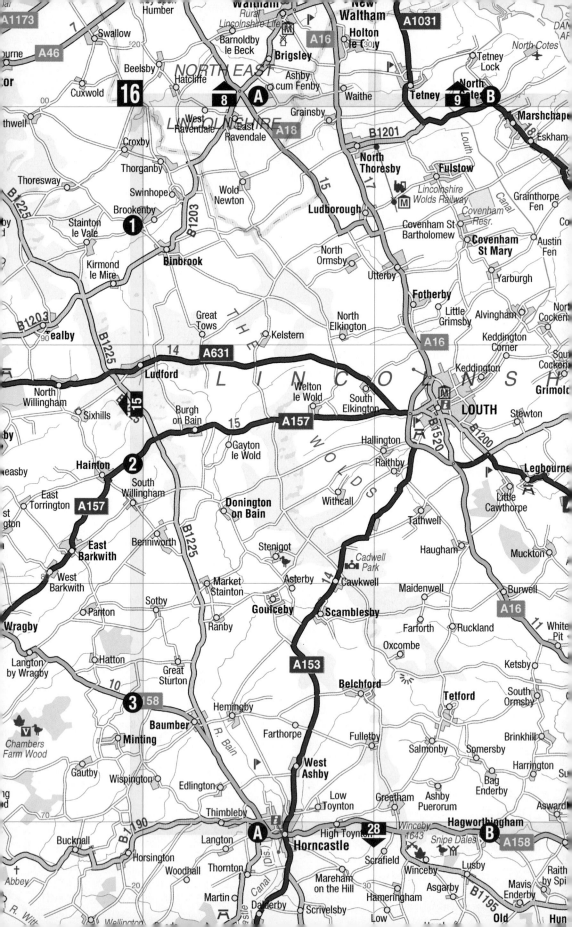

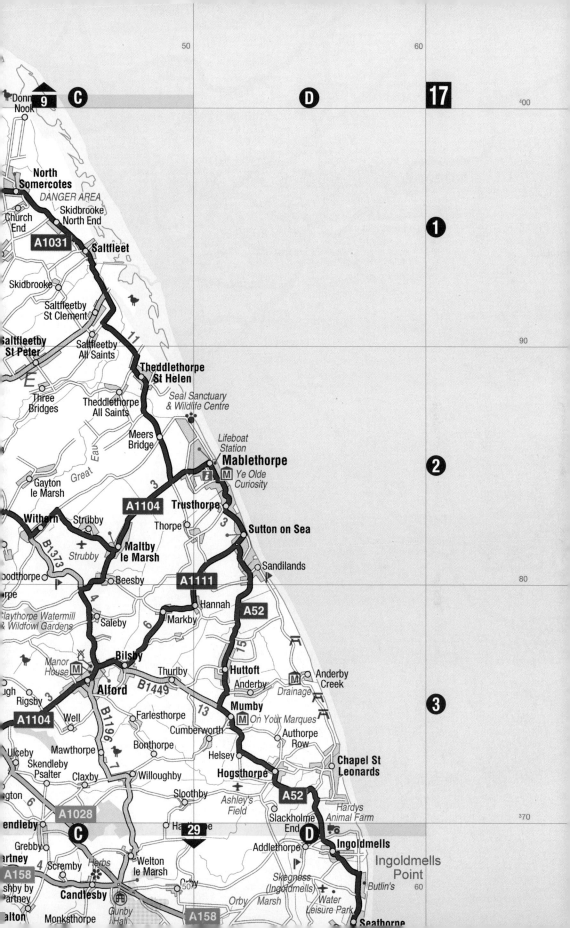

Donna Nook

9

1

North Somercotes

DANGER AREA

Church End

Skidbrooke North End

A1031

Saltfleet

Skidbrooke

Saltfleetby St Clement

Saltfleetby St Peter

Saltfleetby All Saints

11

E

Three Bridges

Theddlethorpe All Saints

Theddlethorpe St Helen

Seal Sanctuary & Wildlife Centre

90

Meers Bridge

Great Eau

Lifeboat Station

Mablethorpe

2

Ye Olde Curiosity

Gayton le Marsh

3

A1104

Trusthorpe

Withern

Strubby

Thorpe

3

Sutton on Sea

B1373

Maltby le Marsh

Strubby

oodthorpe

Beesby

A1111

Sandilands

80

rpe

laythorpe Watermill & Wildfowl Gardens

4

Saleby

6

Hannah

Markby

A52

15

Manor House

Bilsby

Thurlby

Huttoft

Anderby

Anderby Creek

Drainage

3

ugh

Rigsby

3

Alford

B1449

Farlesthorpe

13

Mumby

On Your Marques

A1104

Well

B1196

Cumberworth

Authorpe Row

Ulceby

Mawthorpe

7

Bonthorpe

Helsey

Chapel St Leonards

Skendleby Psalter

Claxby

Willoughby

Hogsthorpe

ngton

6

Sloothby

Ashley's Field

A52

Hardys Animal Farm

³70

ndleby

A1028

C

29

Slackholme End

D

Ingoldmells

Grebby

Welton le Marsh

Addlethorpe

artney

Scremby

Herbs

Orby

Skegness (Ingoldmells)

Ingoldmells Point

Butlin's

60

A158

Candlesby

Gunby Hall

Orby Marsh

Water Leisure Park

alton

Monksthorpe

A158

Seathorpe

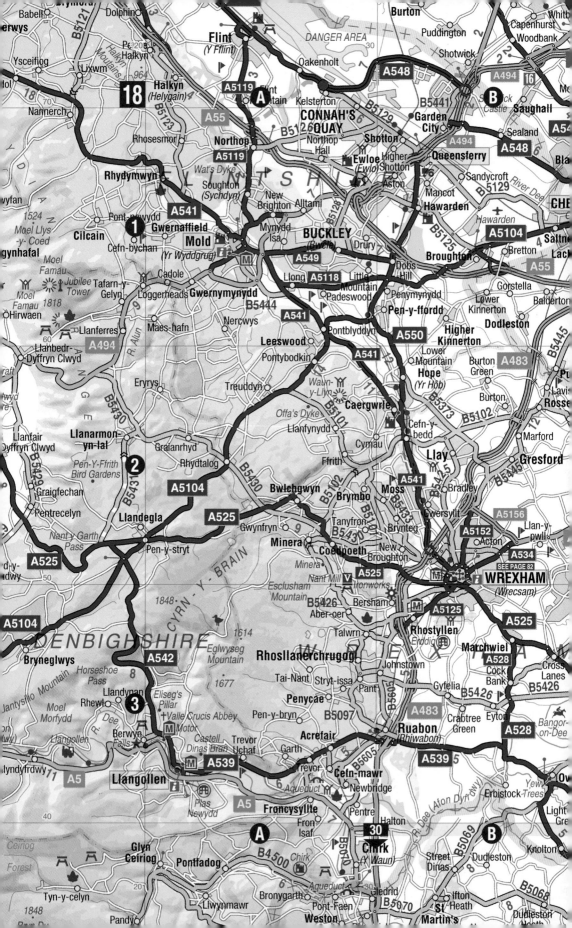

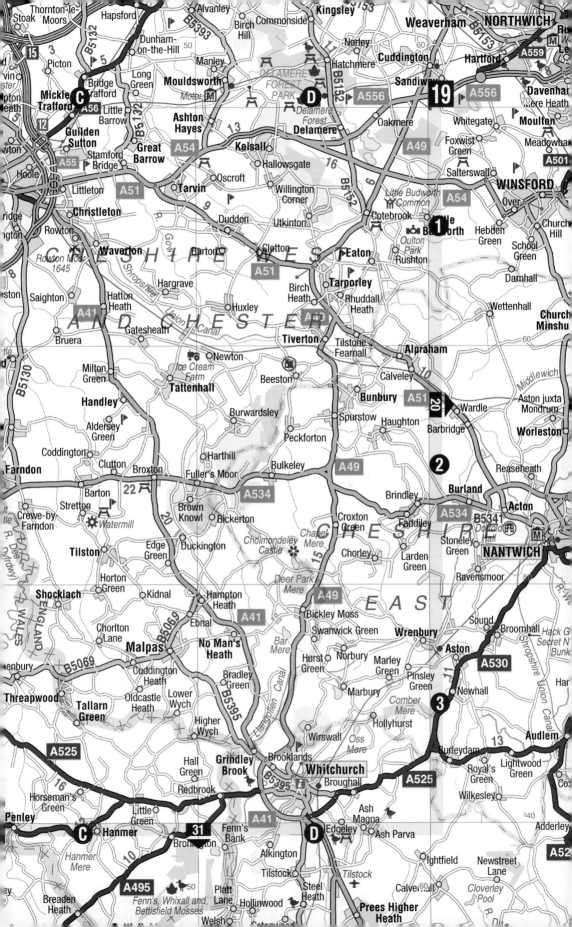

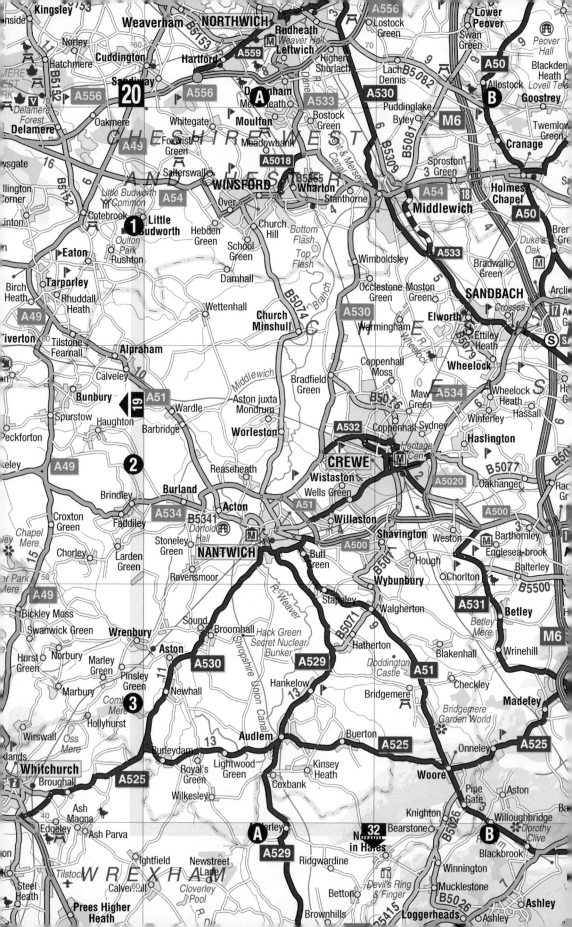

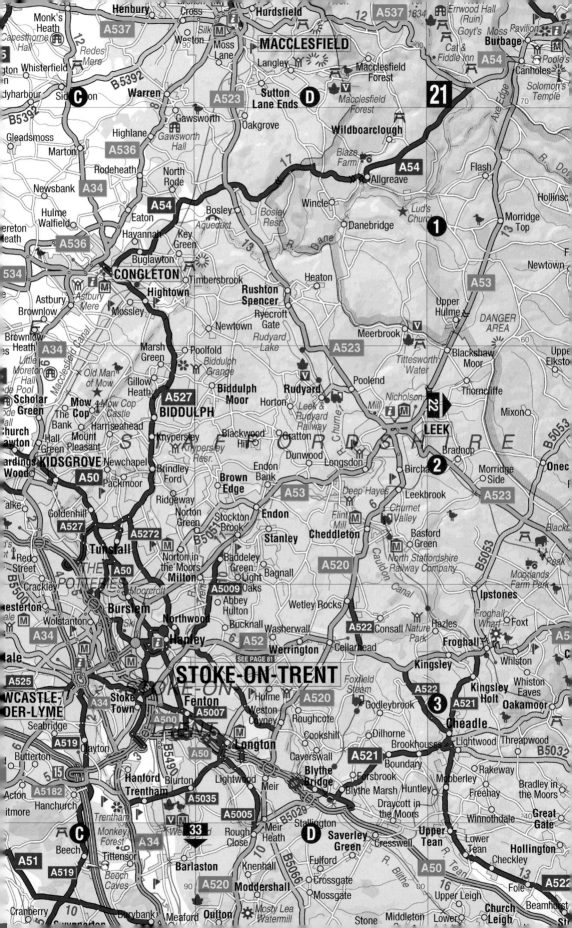

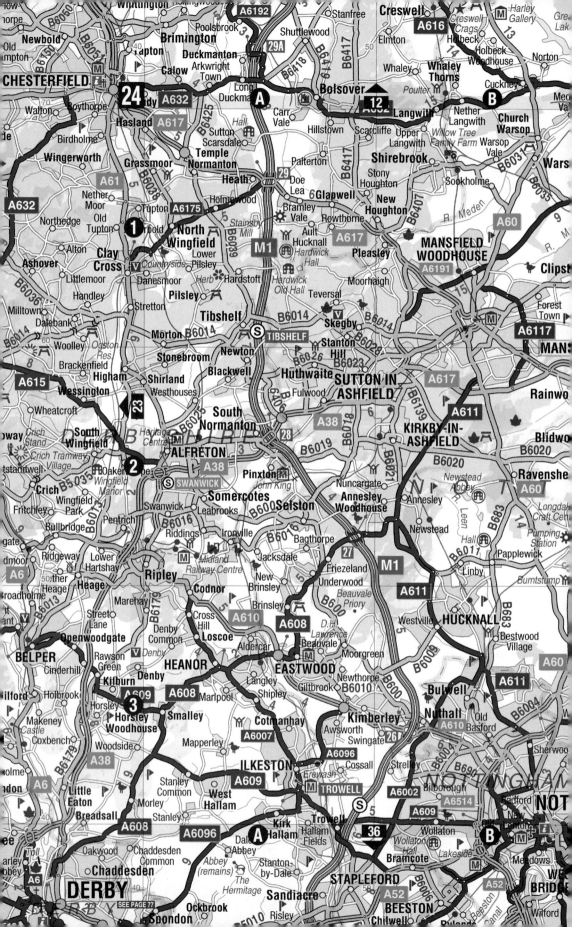

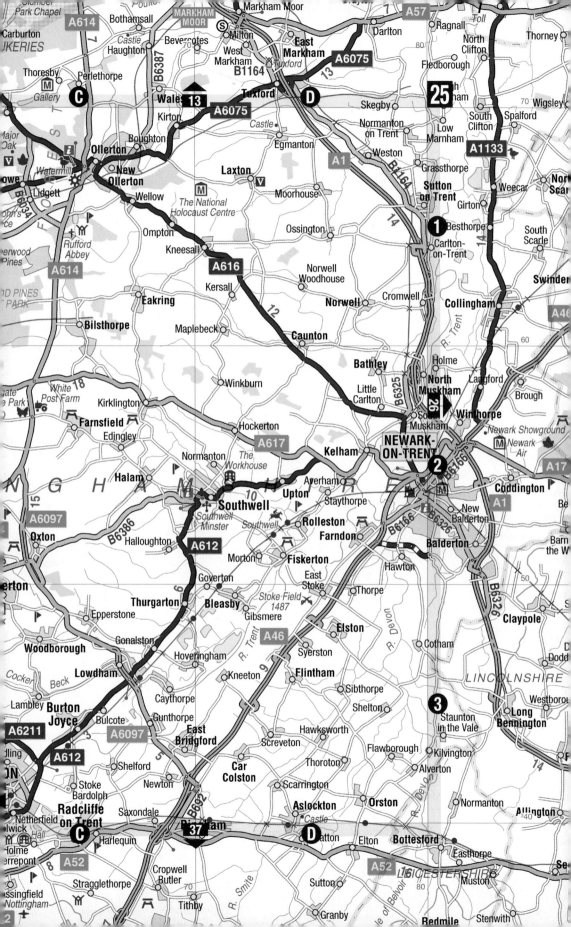

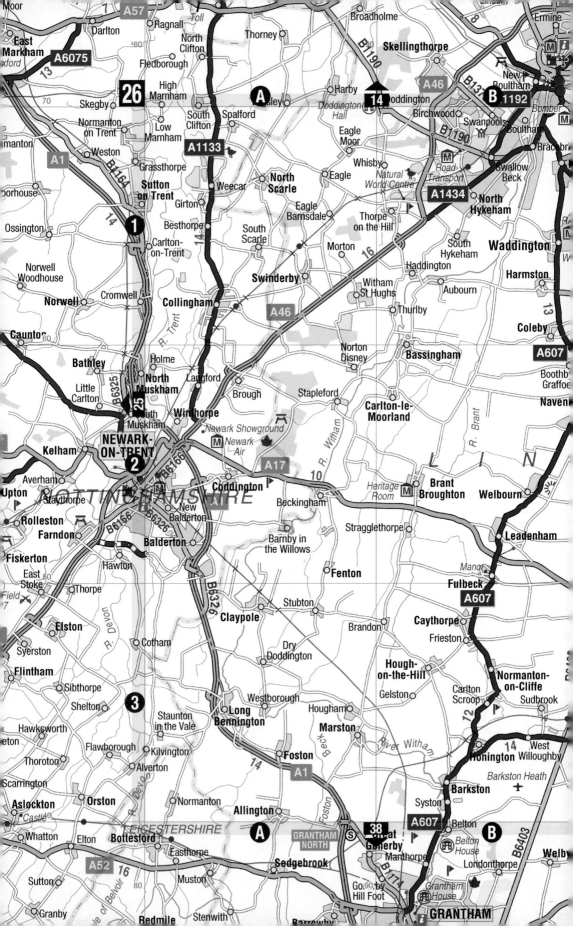

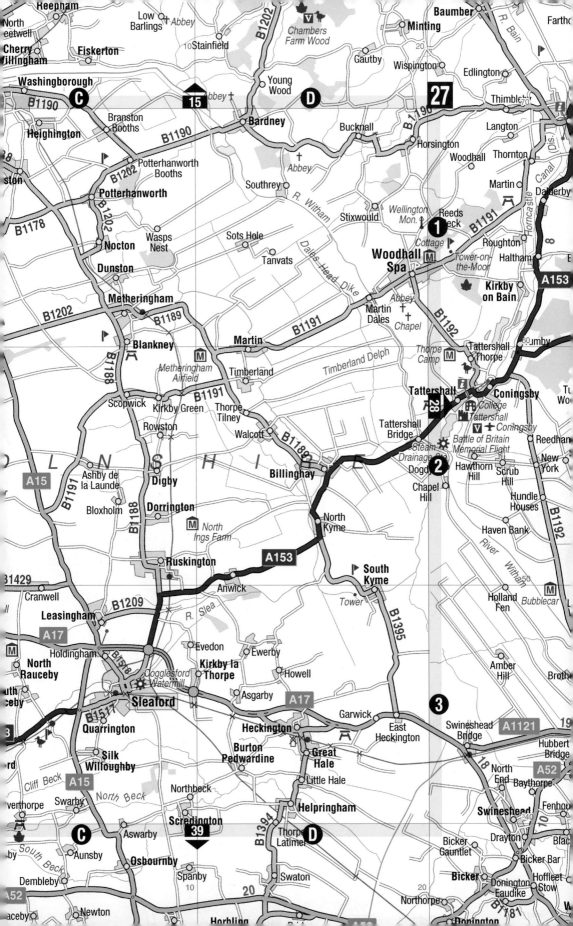

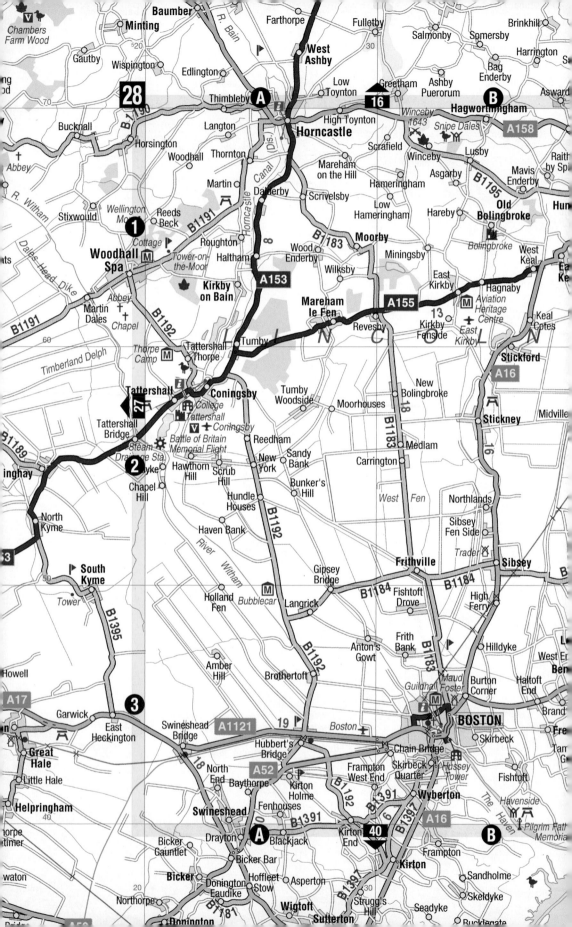

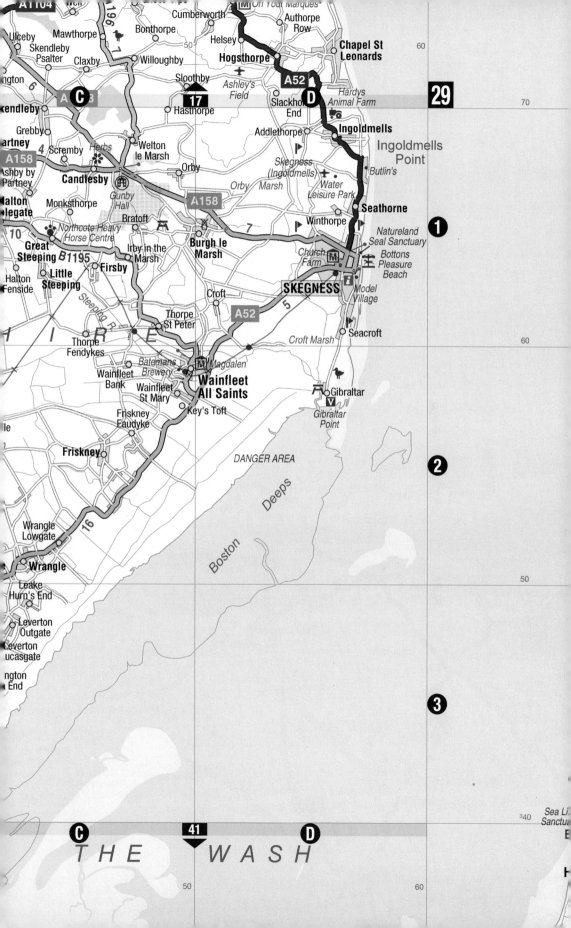

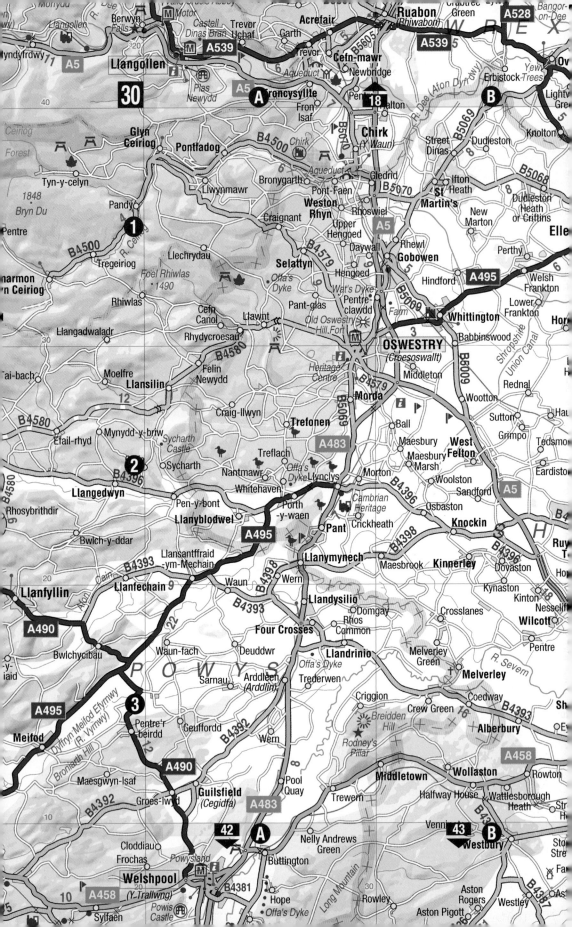

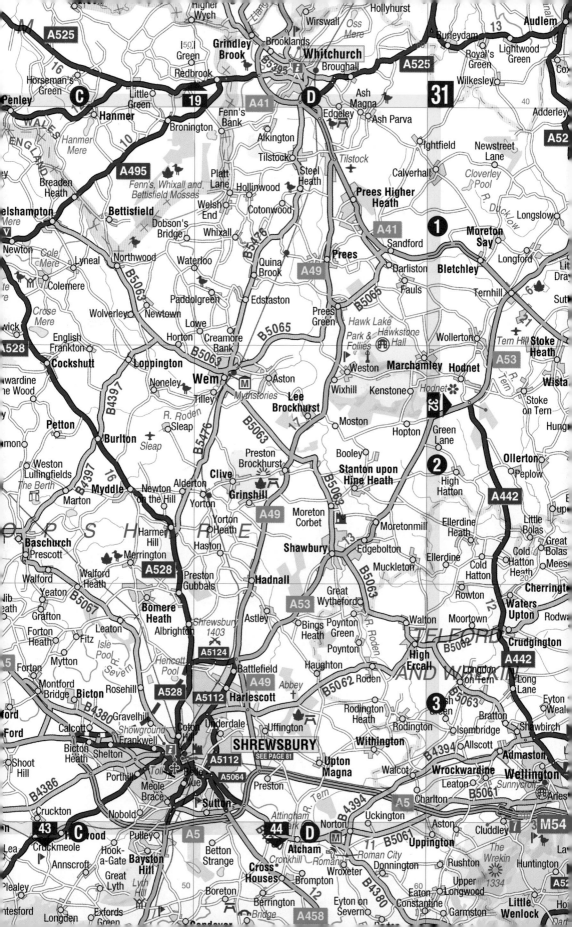

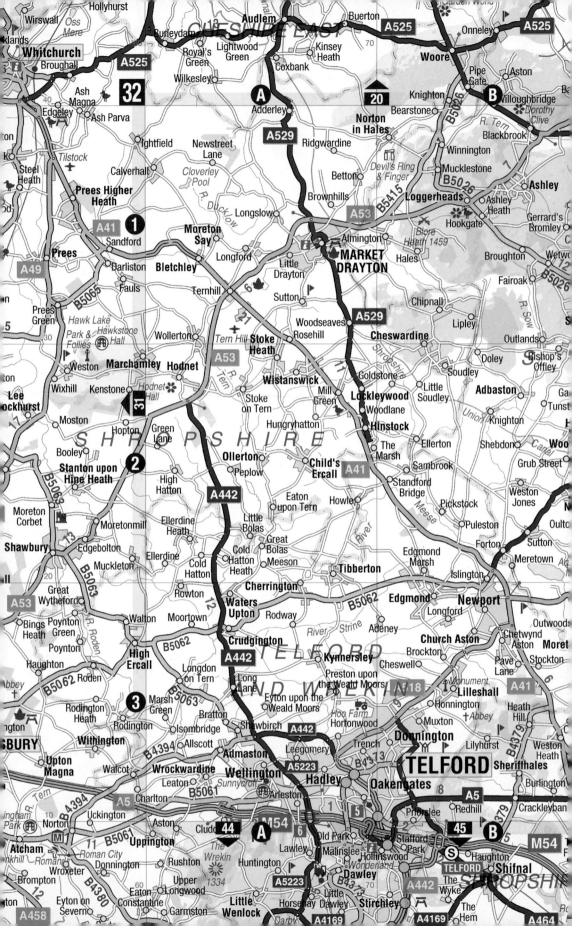

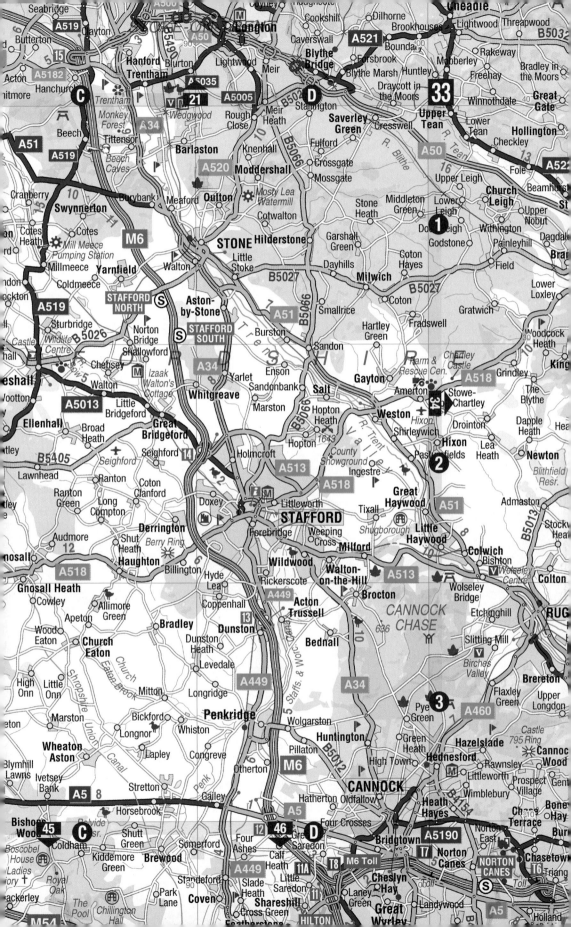

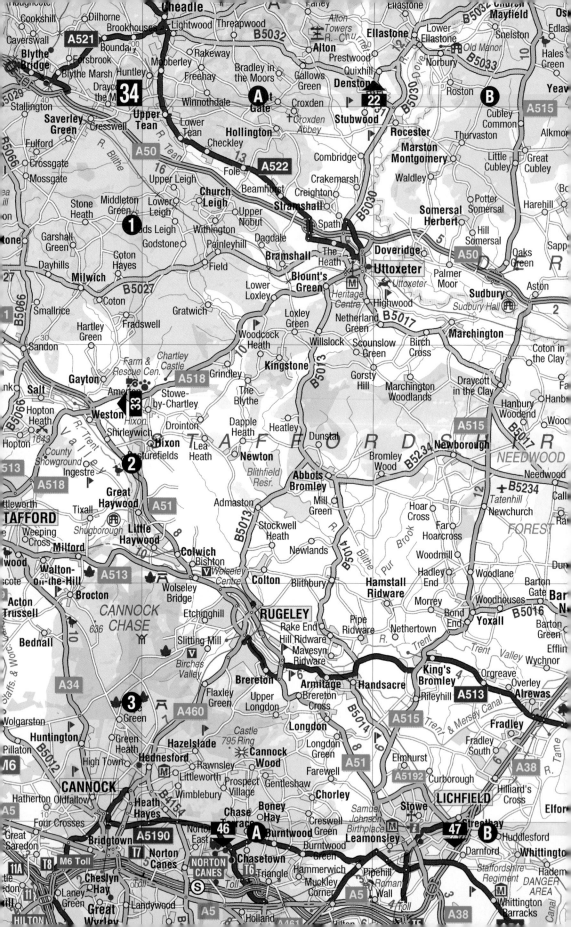

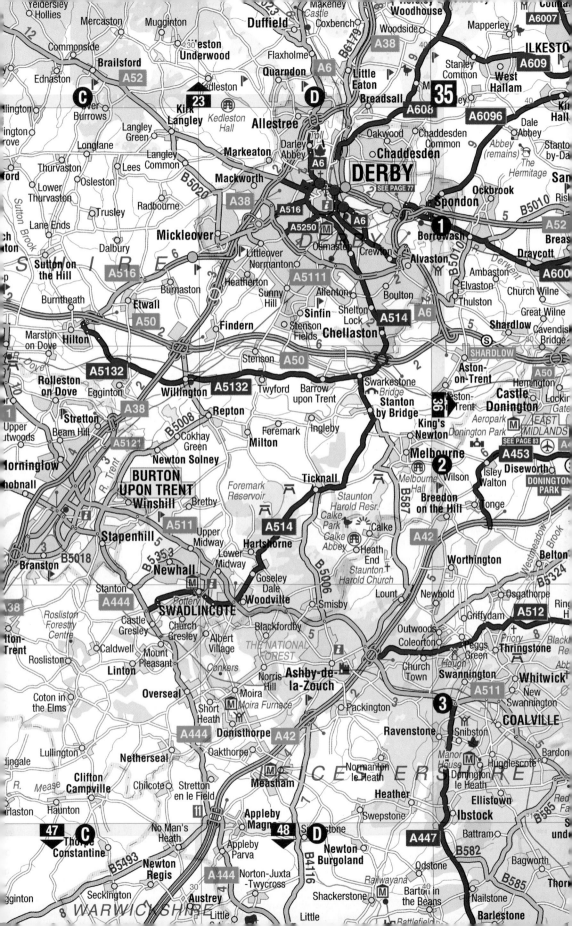

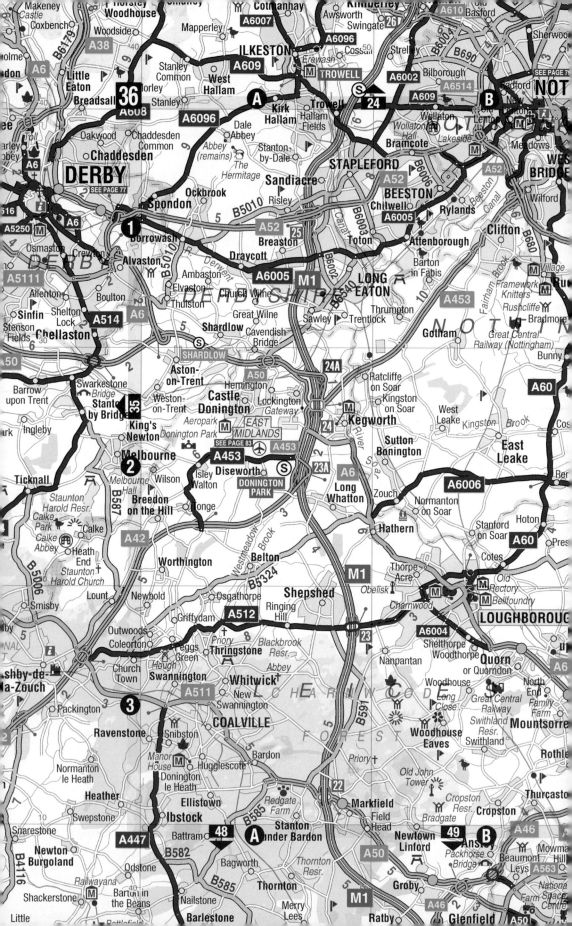

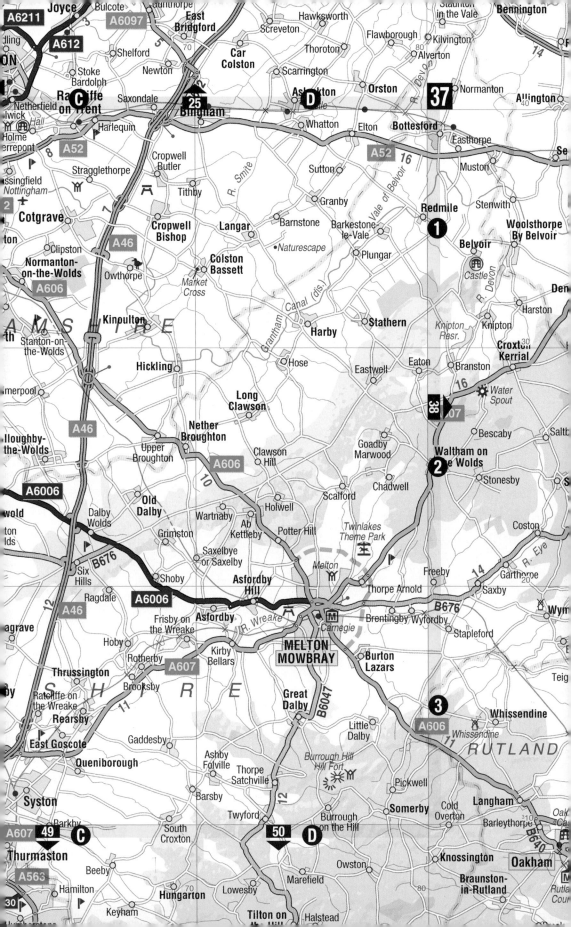

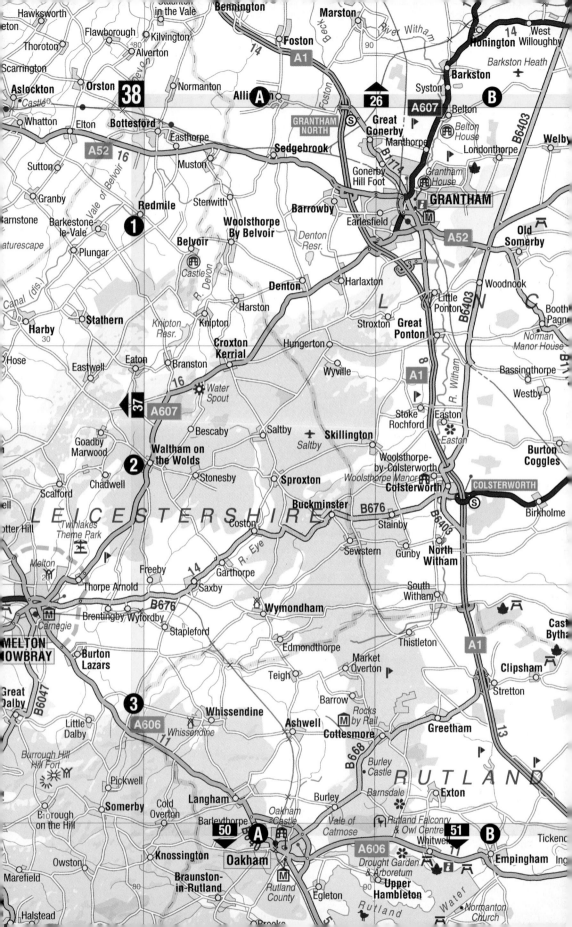

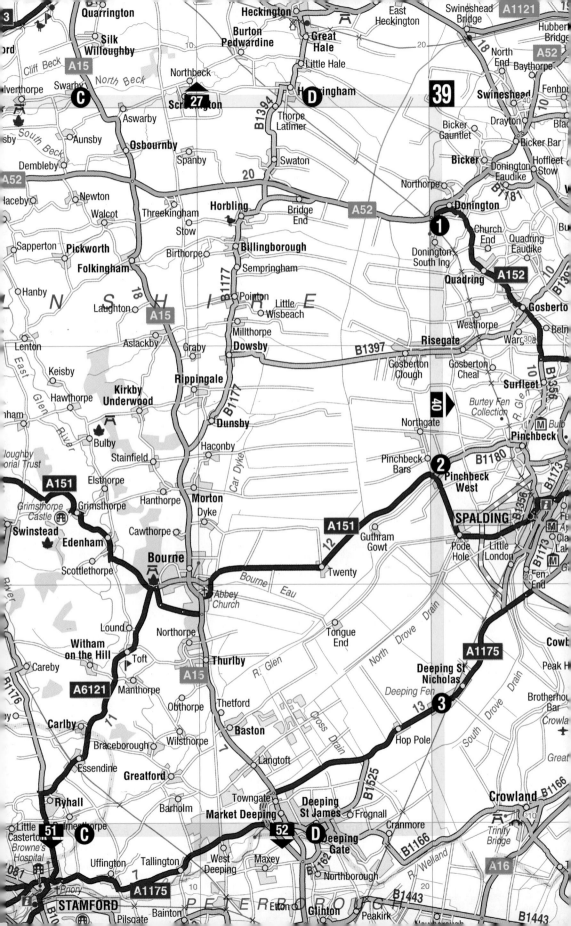

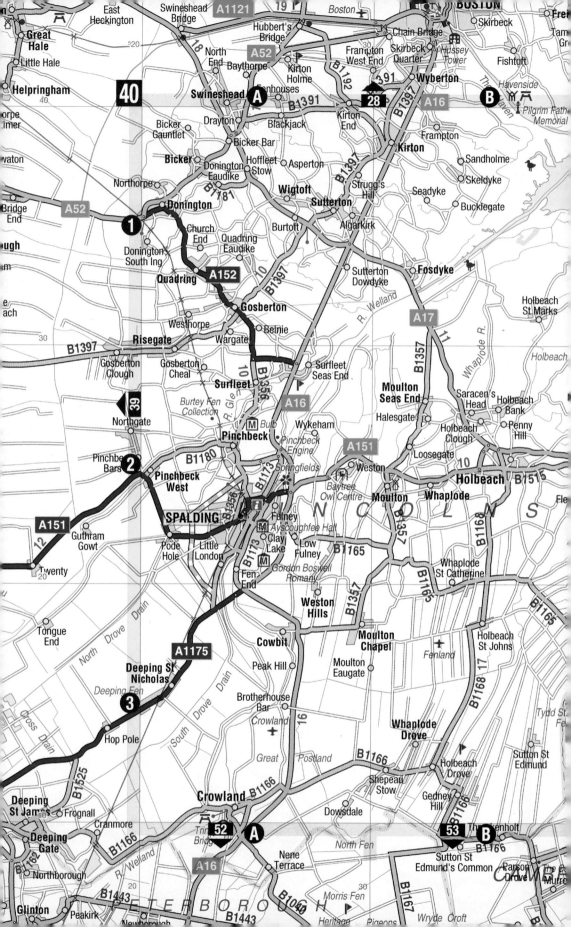

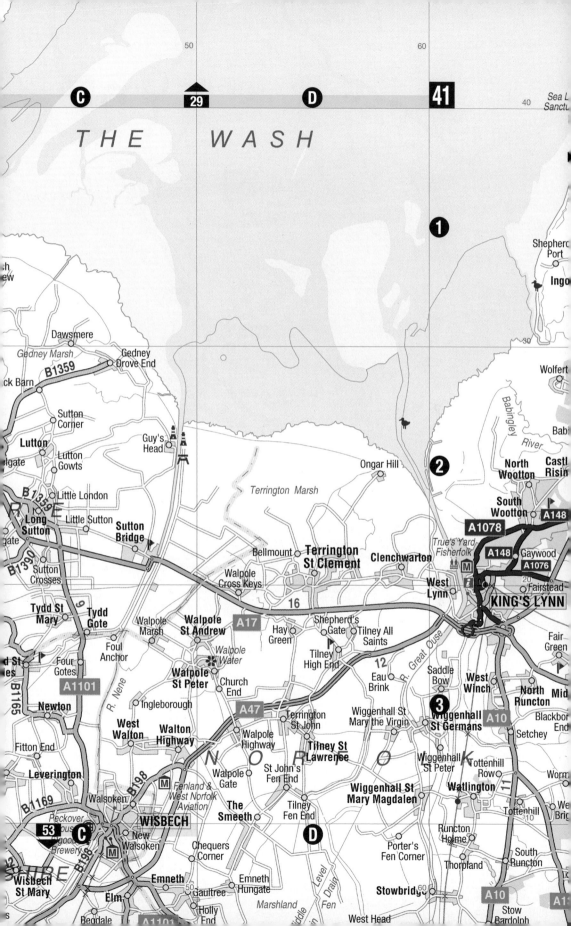

THE WASH

1

Shepherd
Port

Ingo

Dawsmere
Gedney Marsh
ck Barn
Gedney
Drove End
B1359

Wolfert

Babingley River

Bab

Sutton
Corner

Guy's
Head

2

Ongar Hill

**North
Wootton**

**Castl
Risin**

Lutton
gate

Lutton
Gowts

Terrington Marsh

**South
Wootton**

A148

B1359

Little London

**Long
Sutton**

Little Sutton

**Sutton
Bridge**

Bellmount

**Terrington
St Clement**

Clenchwarton

*True's Yard
Fisherfolk*

A1078

A148

A1076

Gaywood

B1390

Sutton
Crosses

Walpole
Cross Keys

M

Fairstead

**West
Lynn**

KING'S LYNN

**Tydd St
Mary**

9

**Tydd
Gote**

Walpole
Marsh

**Walpole
St Andrew**

A17

Hay
Green

Shepherd's
Gate

Tilney All
Saints

16

Fair
Green

d St
es

Foul
Anchor

*Walpole
Water*

Tilney
High End

12

Eau
Brink

Saddle
Bow

**West
Winch**

**North
Runcton**

Mid

Four
Gotes

A1101

**Walpole
St Peter**

Church
End

R. Great Ouse

Newton

Ingleborough

A47

Terrington
St John

Wiggenhall St
Mary the Virgin

3

**Wiggenhall
St Germans**

A10

Blackbor
End

Setchey

**West
Walton**

**Walton
Highway**

Walpole
Highway

**Tilney St
Lawrence**

N   O   R   F   O   L   K

Fitton End

Leverington

Walpole
Gate

St John's
Fen End

Wiggenhall St
Mary Magdalen

Wiggenhall
St Peter

Tottenhill
Row

Worn

B1169

B198

M

*Fenland &
West Norfolk
Aviation*

**The
Smeeth**

Tilney
Fen End

Watlington

Tottenhill

We
Bri

*Peckover
House*

53

C

good
Brewery

M

WISBECH

New
Walsoken

Walsoken

Chequers
Corner

Porter's
Fen Corner

Runcton
Holme

South
Runcton

B198

R. Nene

B1165

**Wisbech
St Mary**

HIRE

Emneth

Elm

Emneth
Hungate

Middle Level Drain

Gaultree

Holly
End

*Marshland
Fen*

West Head

Stowbridge

Thorpland

A10

A1101

Begdale

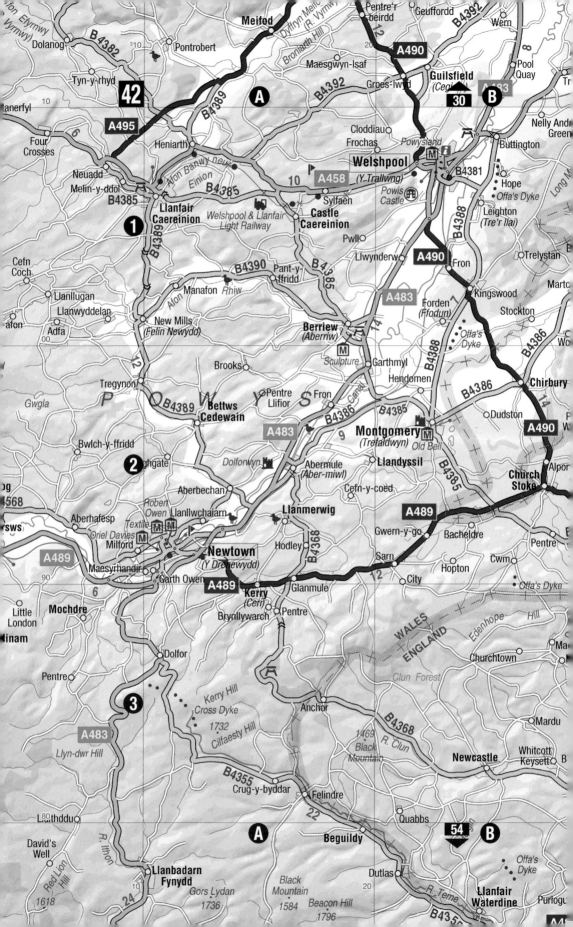

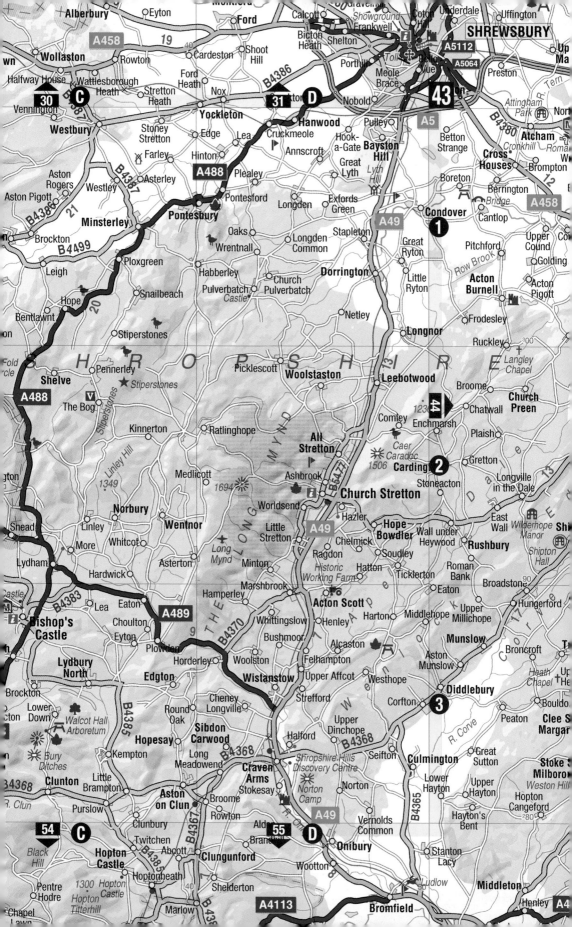

Calcott • Coton Underdale • Uffington • Heath • Rodington • Isombridge • Shawbirch • A442

Frankwell • Cotton Hill • Withington • B4394 • Allscott • Leegomery

SHREWSBURY SEE PAGE 81 • Upton Magna • Walcot • Wrockwardine • Admaston • Wellington • Hadley

Bicton Heath • Shelton • A5112 • A5064 • Preston • B4394 • Uckington • A5 • Charlton • B5061 • Sunnycroft • Arleston

Porthill • Meole Brace • Sutton • 31 • A • Norton • M • 11 • B5061 • Aston • Cluddley • The Wrekin • 32 • 3 • B • M54 • 6 • Old

Hanwood • Pulley • Betton Strange • Atcham • Cronkhill • Roman City • Uppington • Rushton • Huntington • Lawley • Mal

kmeole • Hook-a-Gate • Bayston Hill • Cross Houses • Brompton • Wroxeter • Donnington • Upper Longwood • Little Wenlock • Horsehay • Dawl

Annscroft • Great Lyth • Lyth Hill • Boreton • Berrington • Eyton on Severn • Eaton Constantine • Garmston • A5223 • Darby Houses • Coalbrookdale • Made

Exfords Green • Bridge • Cantlop • Dryton • R. Severn • Leighton • B4380 • Ironbridge • Iron

ngden • Stapleton • A49 • 1 • Condover • Pitchford • Upper Cound • Cound • Harnage • Sheinton • Buildwas • Enginuity • Gorge • Ironbridge

Longden Common • Great Ryton • Golding • Cressage • A4169 • Abbey • Benthall Hall • Benthall • Broseley

Dorrington • Little Ryton • Acton Burnell • Acton Pigott • Harley • Farley • Wyke • Much

rbatch • Netley • Frodesley • Homer • Wenlock • Barrow • B4376

Woolstaston • Longnor • Ruckley • Kenley • The Bank • Priory • Willey

Leebotwood • Langley Chapel • Broome • Church Preen • Hughley • Stretton Westwood • Guildhall • The Smithies

All Stretton • 43 • Comley • Enchmarsh • Chatwall • Plaish • Presthope • Pottery • Atterley • Callaughton

Caer Caradoc • Cardington • Gretton • B4371 • B4318 • Bourton • Muckley • Haughton

Church Stretton • 2 • Stoneacton • Longville in the Dale • Easthope • Acton Round • A458

Hazler • Hope Bowdler • East Wall • Brockton • Weston • B4368 • Astonlane • Morvil

A49 • Chelmick • Wall under Heywood • Wilderhope Manor • Shipton • Upper Netchwood • Aston Eyre • The Lye

Ragdon • Soudley • Rushbury • Shipton Hall • Lower Netchwood • Upton Cressett • Underton

Historic Working Farm • Hatton • Ticklerton • Roman Bank • Broadstone • Stanton Long • Derrington • Middleton Priors • Chetton • The Down

Acton Scott • Harton • Eaton • Hungerford • Holdgate • Ashfield • Hillside • Ditton Priors • Neenton • Middleton Scriven

yslow • Henley • Middlehope • Upper Millichope • Tugford • Abdon • Cleobury North • Wrickton • Overton

Alcaston • Westhope • Munslow • Broncroft • Heath Chapel • Upper Heath • Burwarton • The Highlands • Sidb

Felhampton • Aston Munslow • Diddlebury • Bouldon • Cockshutford • Nordy Bank • Aston Botterell • Stottesdon

Strefford • Corfton • 3 • Peaton • Clee St Margaret • Brown • Loughton • Wheathill

Upper Dinchope • B4368 • Great Sutton • Stoke St Milborough • Blackford • Bromdon • Farlow • Oreton

Halford • Seifton • Culmington • Lower Hayton • Upper Hayton • Weston Hill • Hopton Cangeford • Cleedownton • Silvington • Crumpsbrook • Catherton

Shropshire Hills Discovery Centre • Norton • Hayton's Bent • 55 • A • Cleestanton • 56 • B

Norton Camp • A49 • Vernolds Common • Stanton Lacy • Cleestanton • Titterstone Clee Hill • Cleeton St Mary • Neen Savage

Onibury • Ludlow • Middleton • Bitterley • Angelbank • Doddington • Foxwood • Hopton Wafers • Cleobury Mortimer

Wootton • Bromfield • Henley • A4117 • Clee Hill

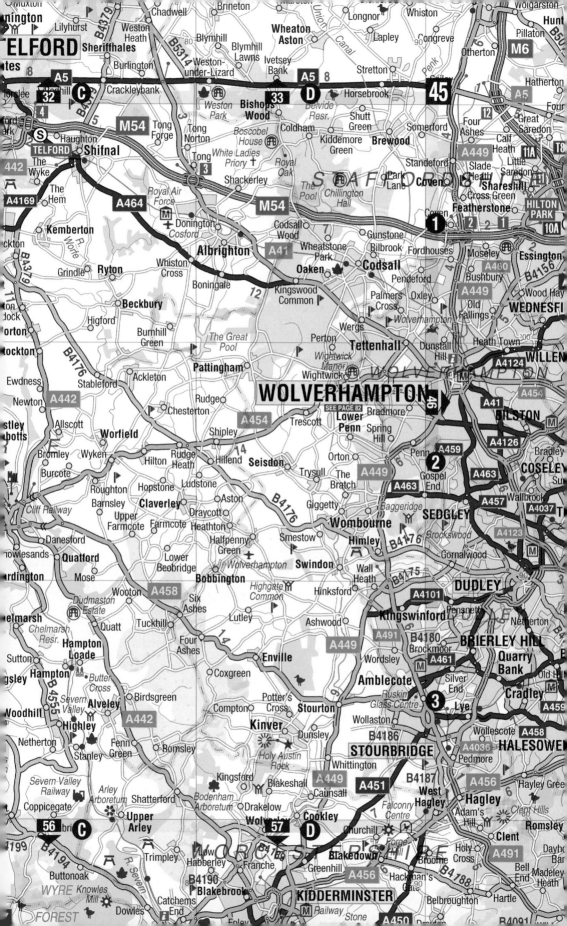

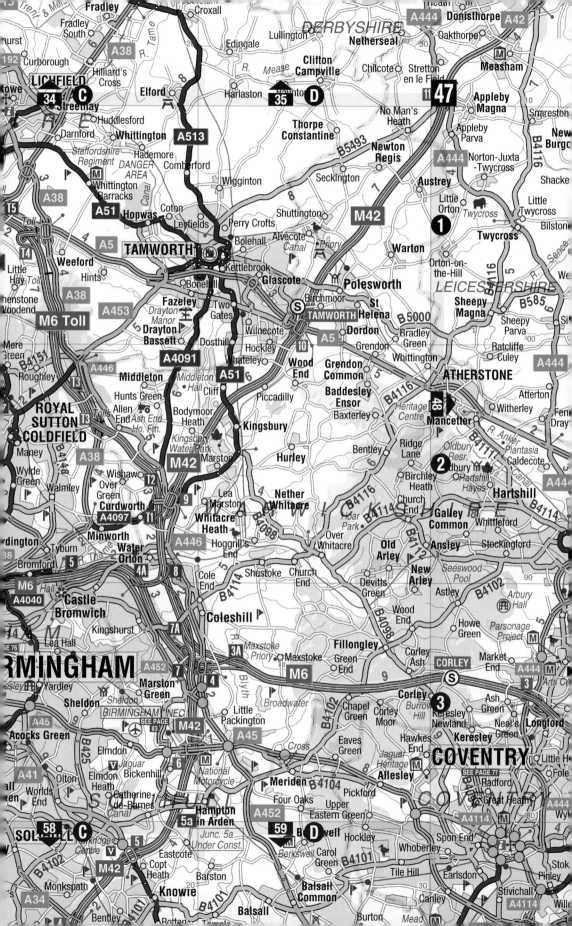

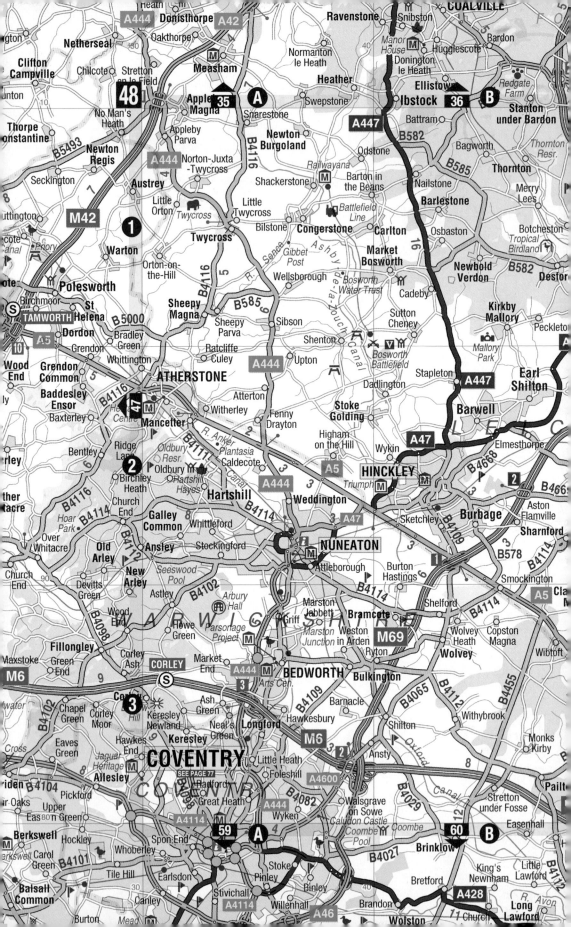

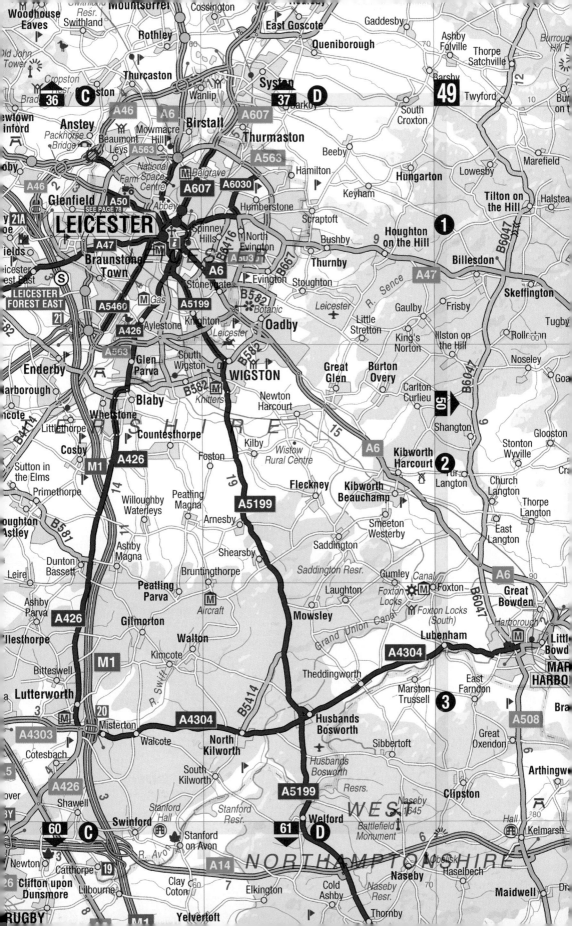

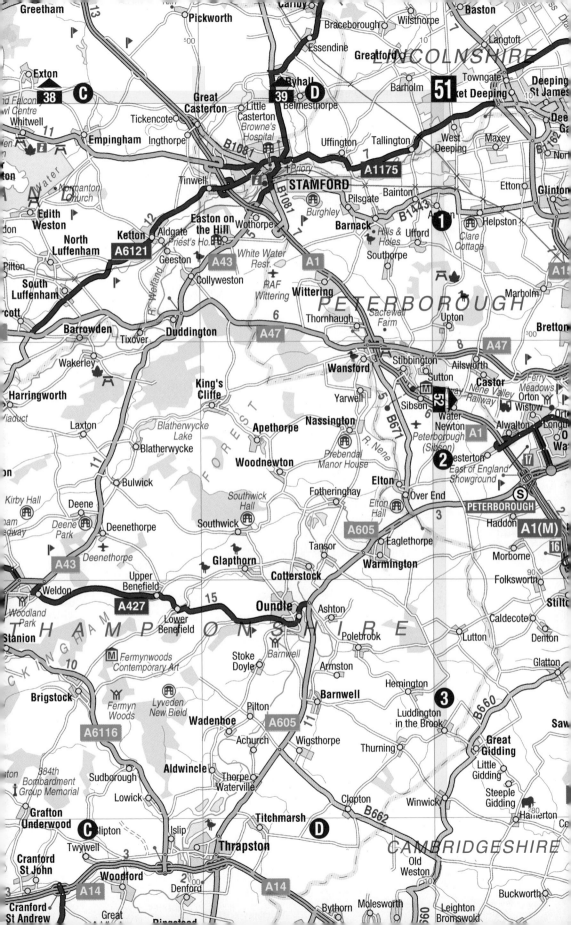

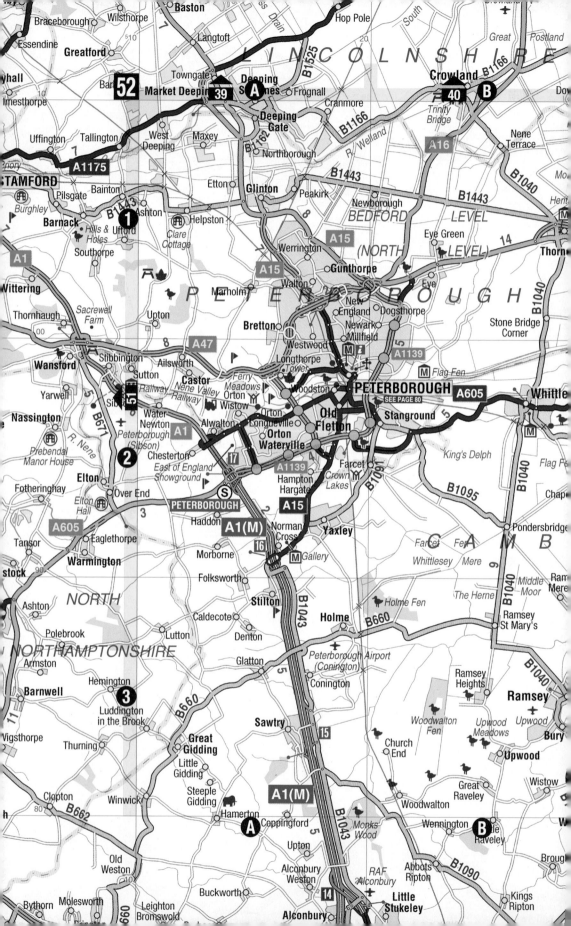

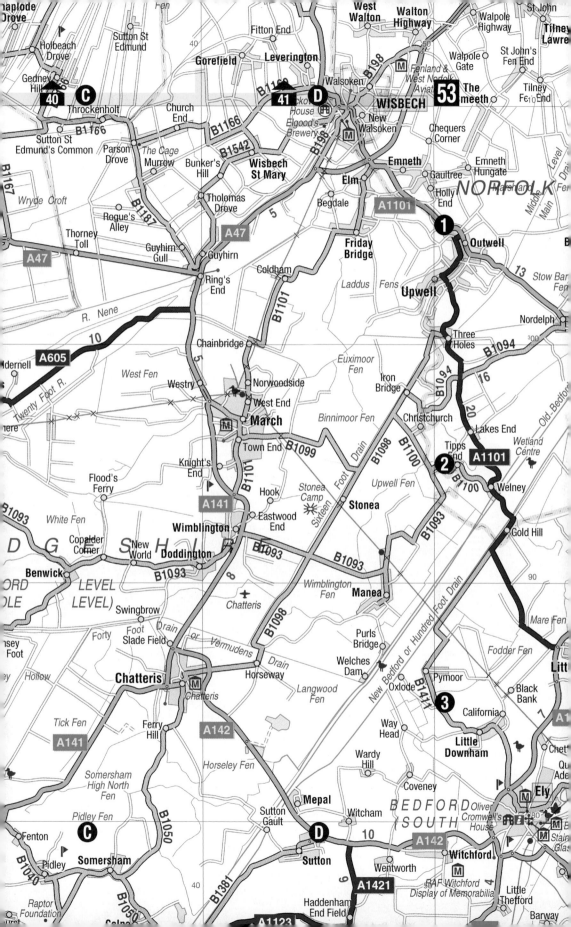

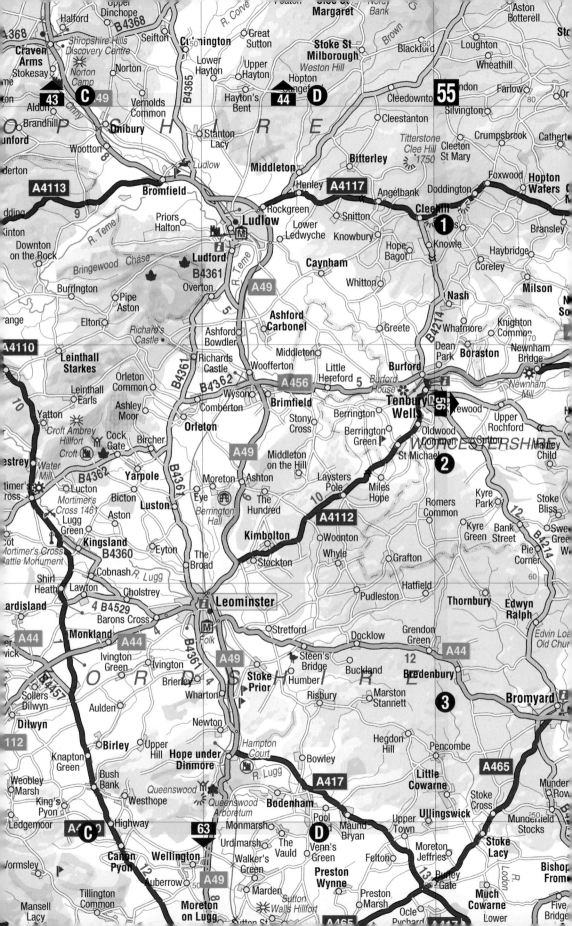

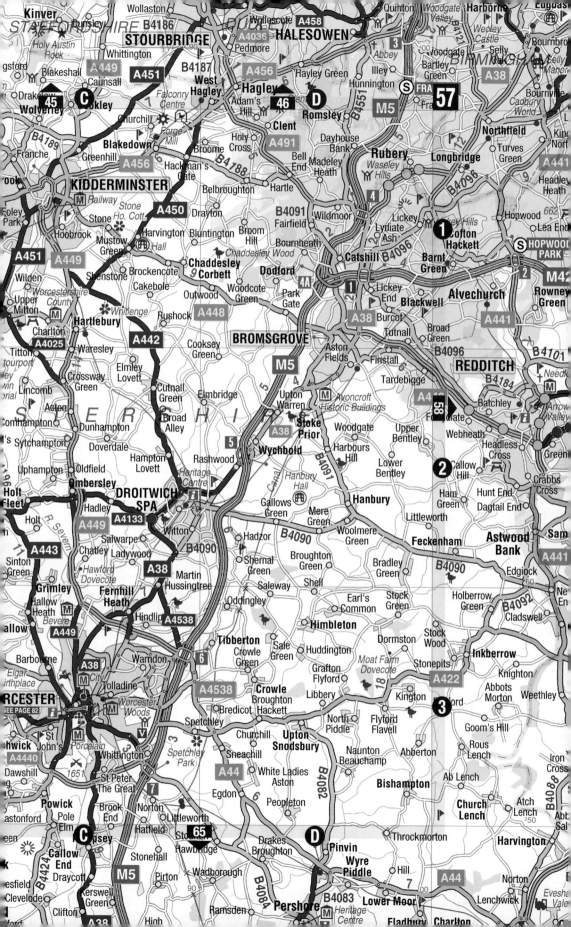

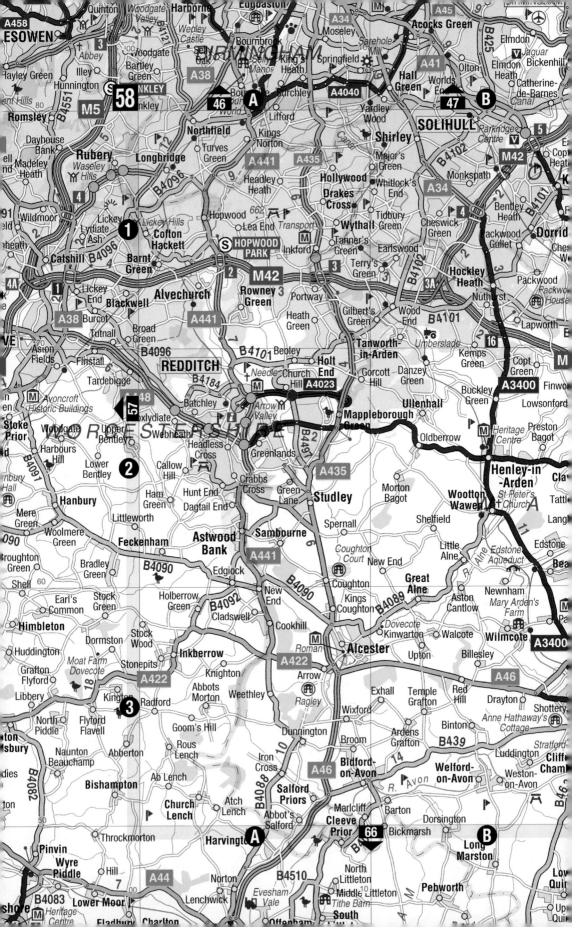

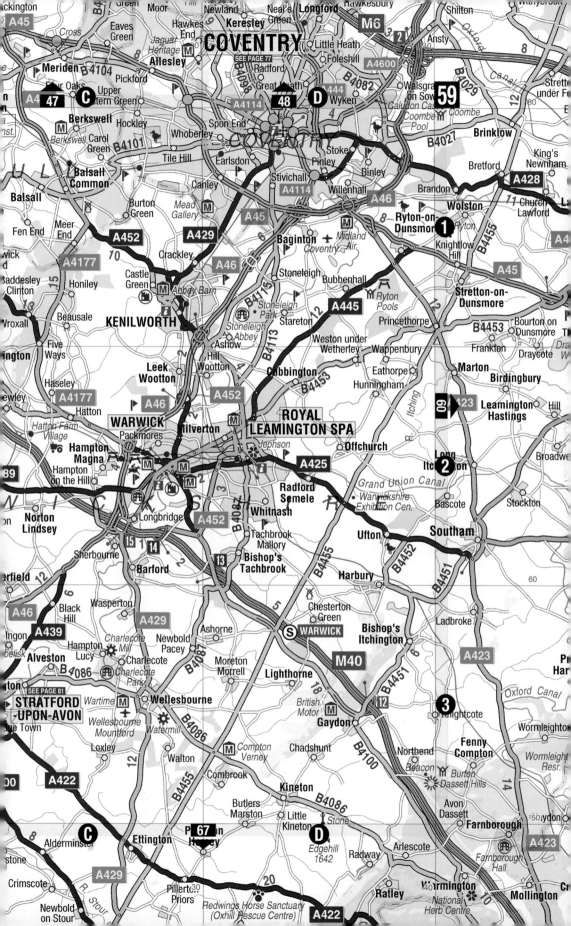

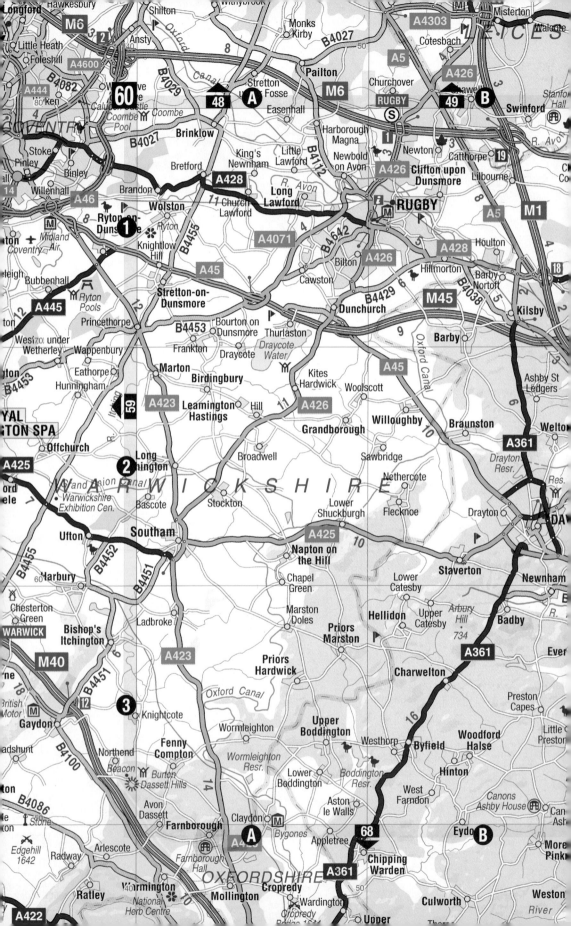

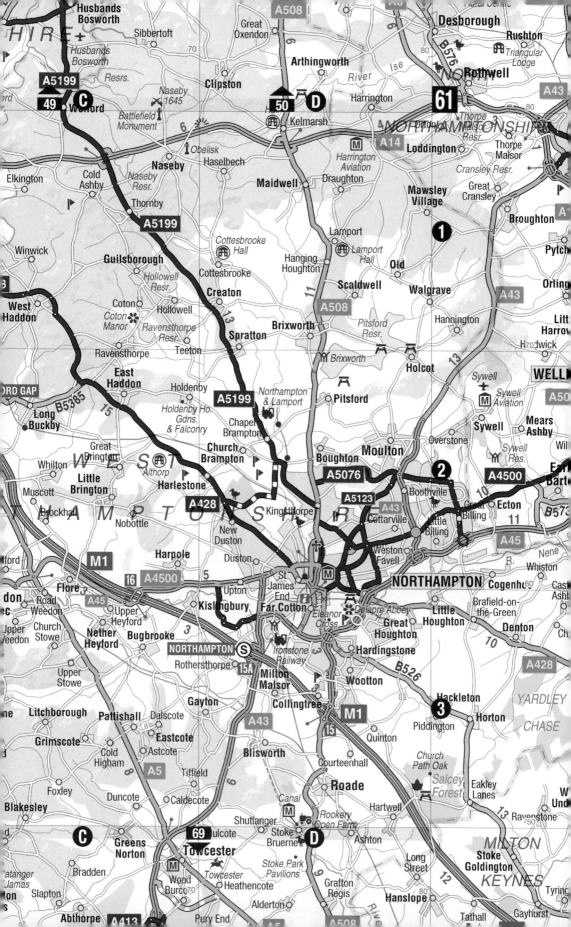

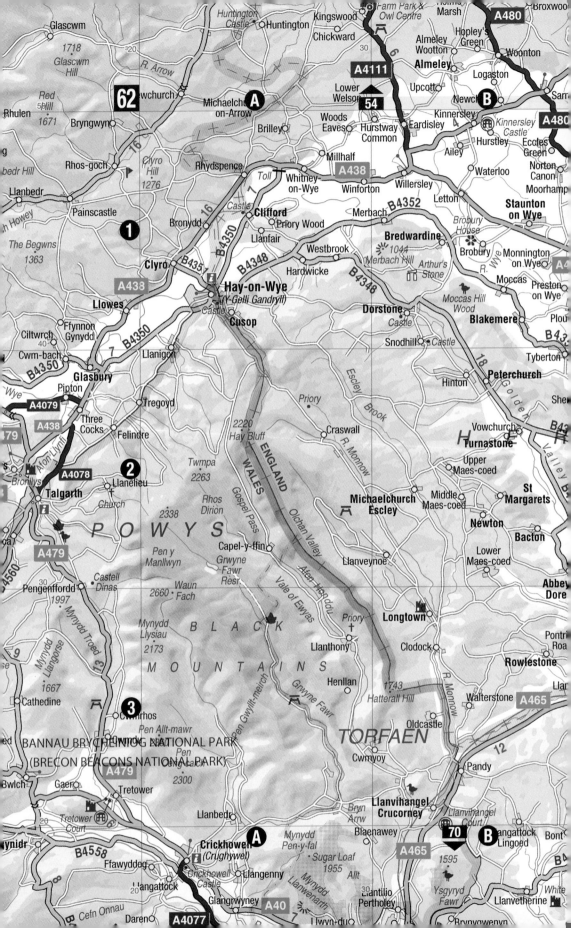

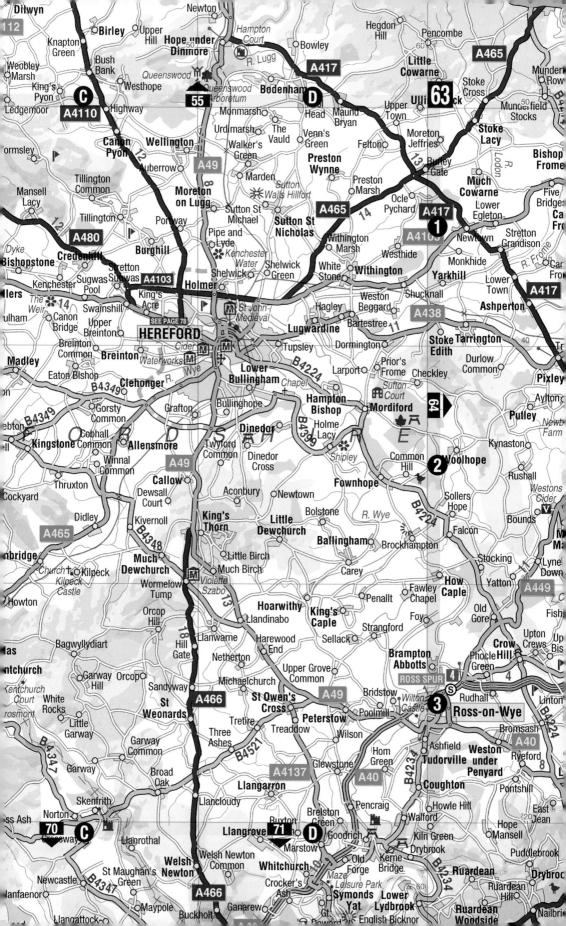

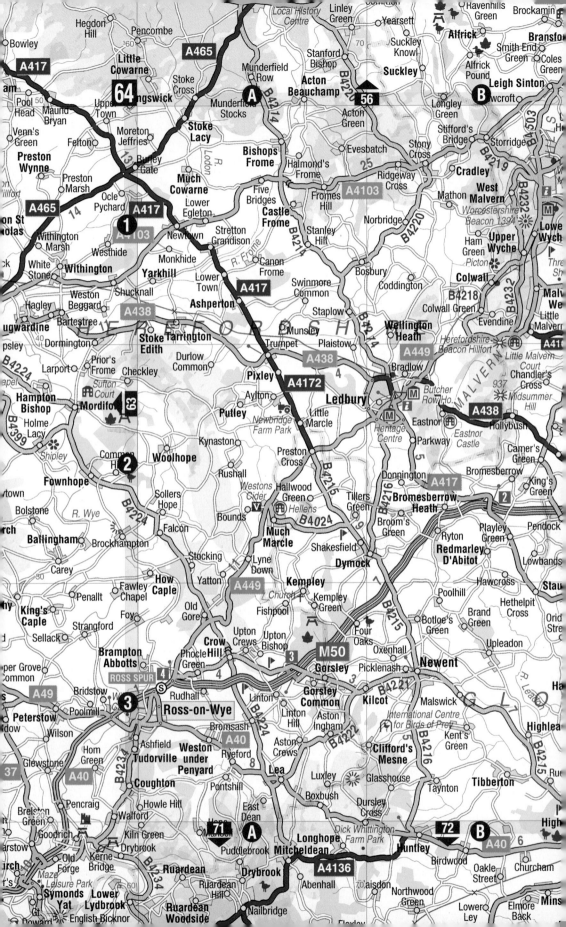

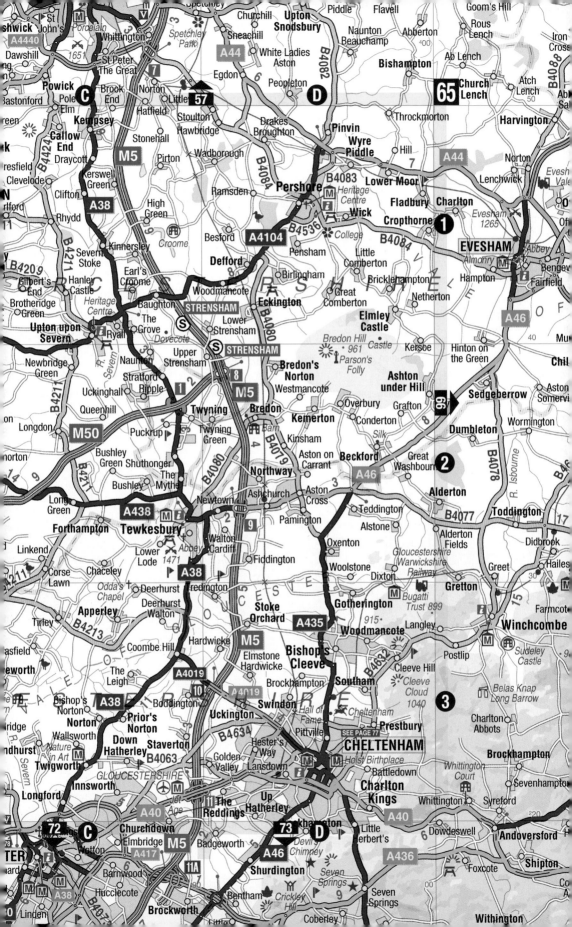

Piddle Flavell Goom's Hill Dunnington Broom Ardens Grafton Binton Cottage
ton sbury Naunton Beauchamp Abberton Rous Lench Iron Cross A46 B439 Luddington Stratford Cliffo Cham
dies B4082 Ab Lench Atch Lench Salford Priors Bidford-on-Avon 14 Welford-on-Avon Weston-on-Avon Chaml

66 Bishampton Church Lench **A** Abbot's Salford Marlcliff Cleeve Prior **58** Barton Dorsington **B** B46
ton Throckmorton Harvington Bickmarsh Long Marston

Pinvin Wyre Piddle Hill 7 A44 Norton Lenchwick North Littleton Middle Littleton Pebworth Low Quin
shore B4083 Lower Moor Charlton B4510 Evesham Vale Tithe Barn South Littleton Broad Marston 14 Upp Qui
Heritage Centre Wick Fladbury Cropthorne **1** Evesham 1265 Offenham 636 Meon Hill

Little Comberton EVESHAM Almonry Offenham Cross Bretforton Honeybourne Mickleton Kitsgate Court Hidc Bartri
ngham Bricklehampton Hampton Bengeworth Fairfield Badsey Aston Subedge B4035 B4632 Hidc Boyc
Great Comberton Netherton Aldington B4081 Hidc

Elmley Castle Kersoe Hinton on the Green Wickhamford A44 Willersey Weston-sub-Edge Chipping Campden Ebrin
on's Bredon Hill 961 Castle Murcot 6 B4632 Saintbury Market Hall Ernest Wilson Memorial
ton Parson's Folly Childswickham Littleworth Broad Campden

Ashton under Hill **65** Sedgeberrow Aston Somerville Broadway Bury End Broadway Tower Blockley Draycot Batsford Arboretum
mancote Overbury Grafton 8 Dumbleton Wormington Buckland Mill Dene B4419
sham Conderton Silk Beckford **2** Gre Wash one B4078 Laverton B4632 Snowshill Manor Snowshill A44 Bourton-on-the-Hill Cots Falcor
Aston on Carrant Alderton Stanton Bourton Ho. Sezin
Aston Cross Teddington B4077 Toddington 17 Stanway Stanway House & Fountain Taddington A424 Longbo
ngton Alstone Alderton Fields Didbrook Hinchwick
Oxenton Woolstone Gloucestershire Warwickshire Railway Greet Hailes Wood Stanway Cutsdean Condicote Donnir
Dixton Gretton Hailes Abbey Ford Ganborough A424
Gotherington Bugatti Trust 899 Farmcote Hyde Hinchwick Temple Guiting B4077 Upper Swell
A435 Woodmancote Langley Winchcombe 15 Farmcote Kineton Cotswold Farm Park Lower Swell Old Mill A429
hops Postlip Sudeley Castle 982 Belas Knap Long Barrow Barton Chalk Hill Upper Slaughter Model Village Ris
leeve Cleeve Hill GLOUCESTERSHIRE Lower Slaughter
mpton Southam Cleeve Cloud 10 **3** Charlton Abbots Guiting Power Naunton B4068 Bourton-the-W
Hall of Fame Cheltenham 915 Prestbury Brockhampton Hawling Upper Slaughter Model Railway Exhibition Netherc
ttville SEE PAGE 77 Whittington Court 863 Aylworth 12 Birdland Park & Gardens Ris
CHELTENHAM Holst Birthplace Sevenhampton Notgrove Long Barrow Cotswold A436
Charlton Kings Battledown Whittington Syreford Salperton Cots Aston
hampton Little Herbert's A40 Dowdeswell **73** **A** Hampen Notgrove Cole Aston **74** **B** Bourt
evil's imney A436 Andvers Hazleton Model Village
Seven Springs Foxcote Shipton 841 Turkdean Clapton-on-the-Hill
Coberley 9 Seven Springs Compton Abdale A40 Farmington R.
Withington

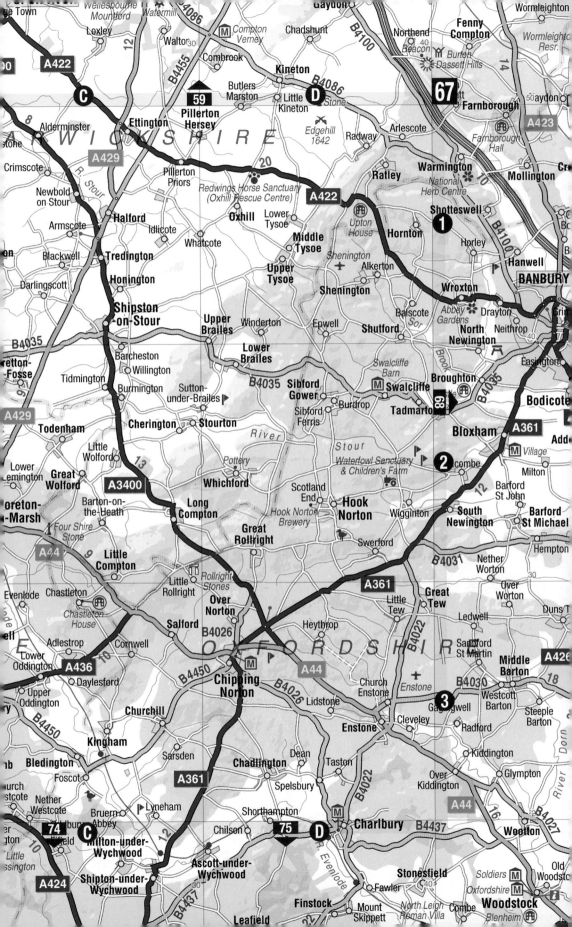

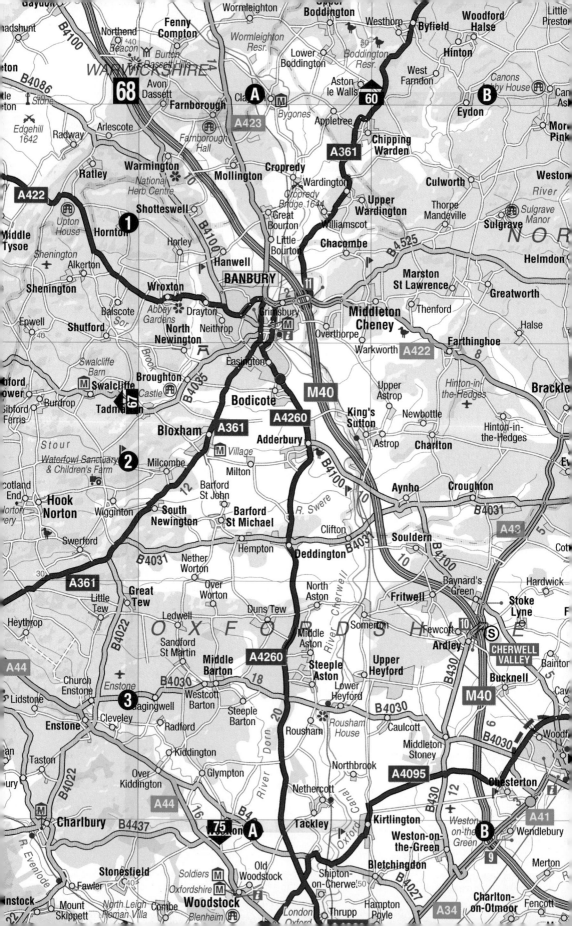

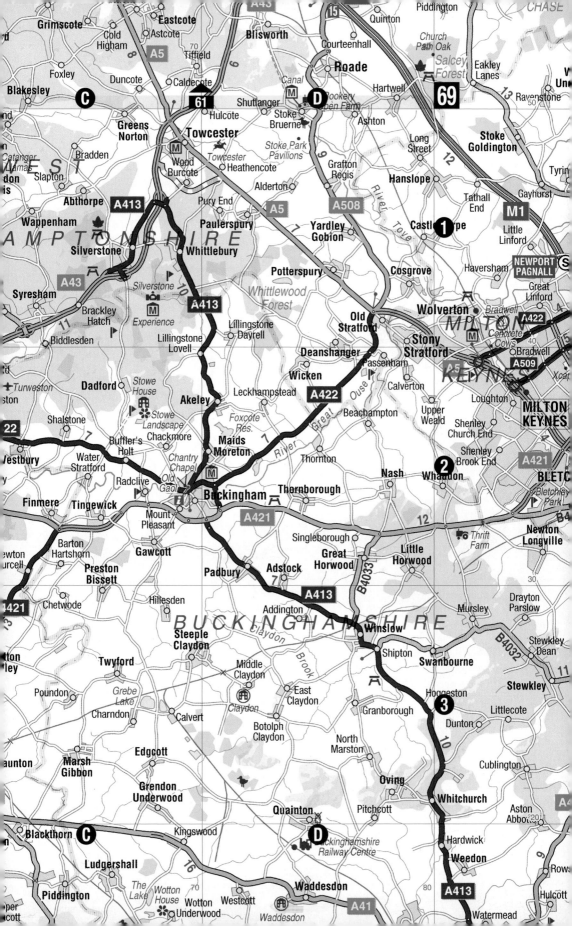

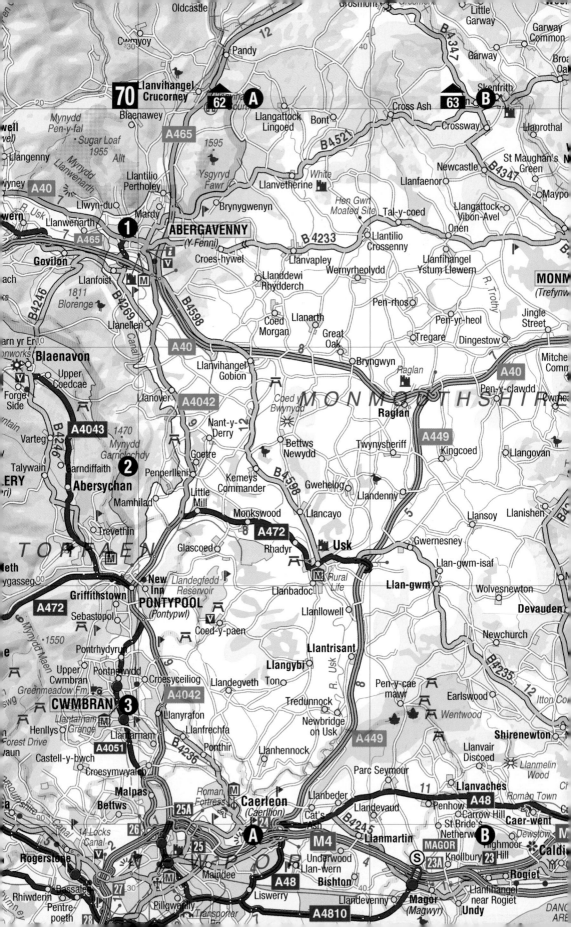

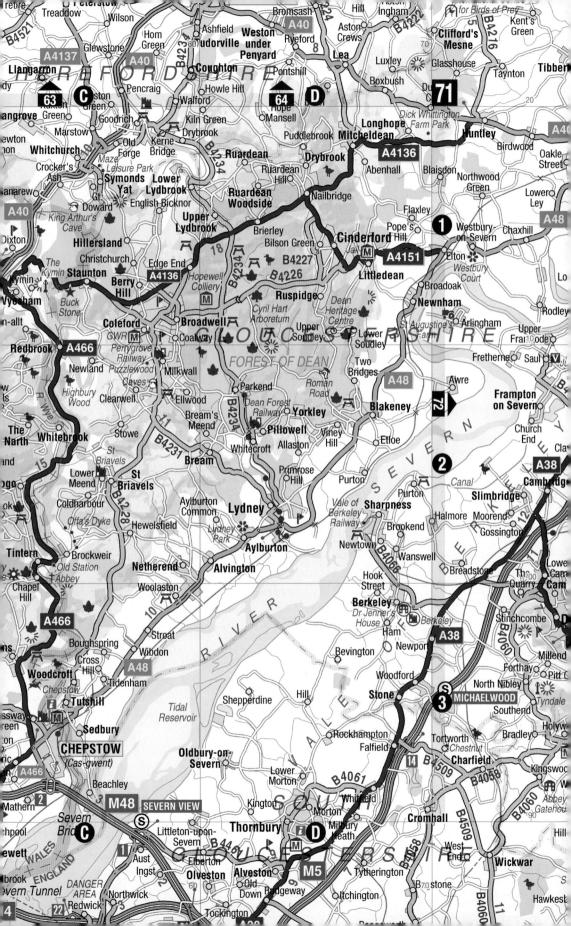

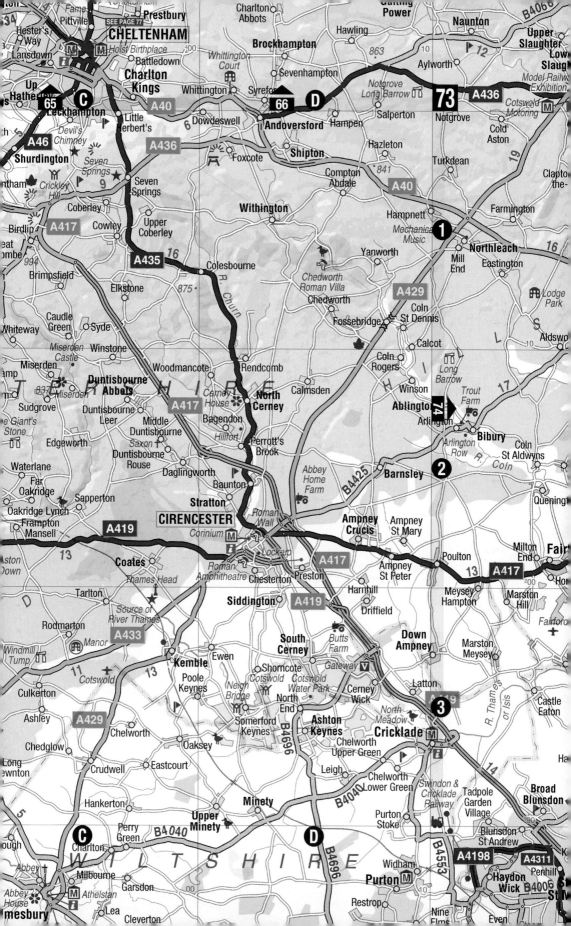

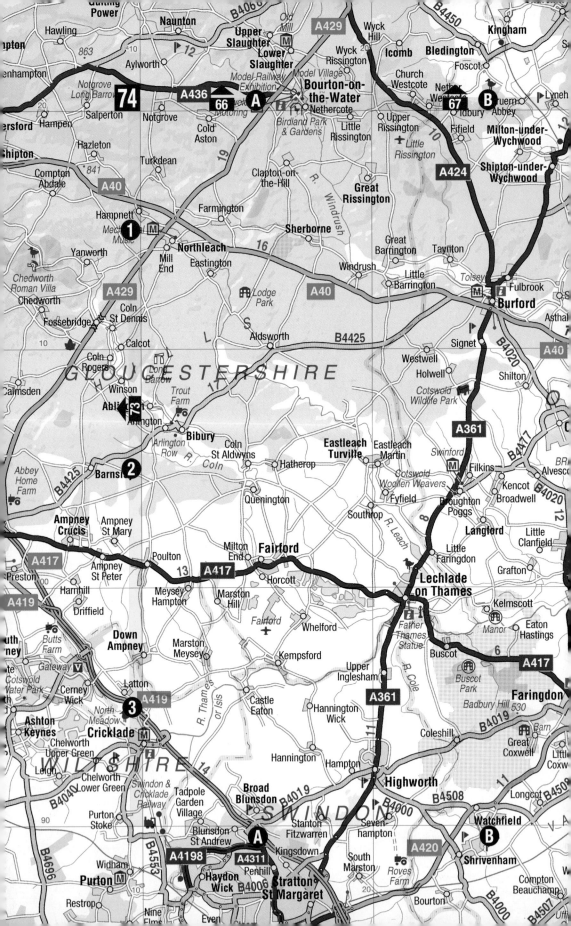

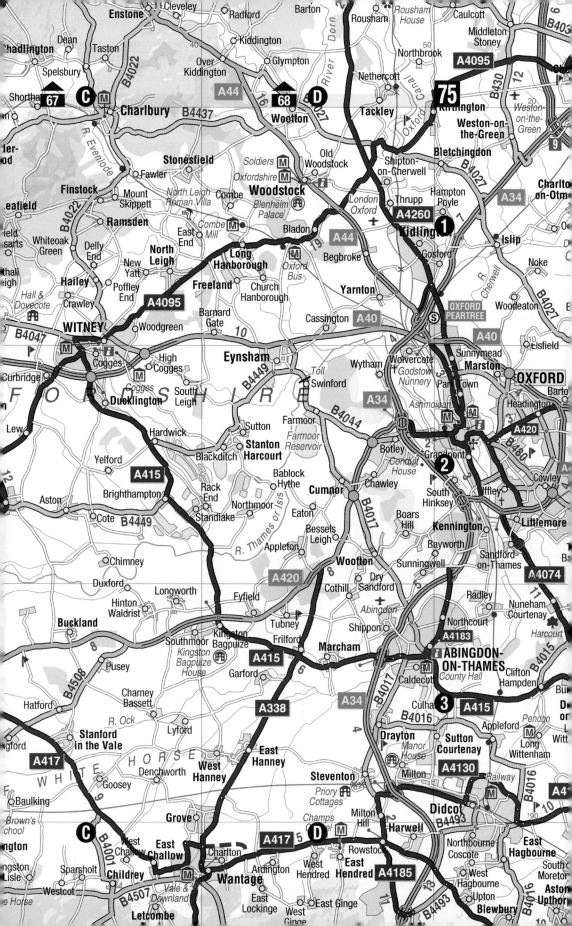

CITY & TOWN CENTRE PLANS

Reference to Town Plans

Motorway	**M1**	Abbey, Cathedral, Priory etc.	✝
Motorway Under Construction		Bus Station	⊶
Motorway Junctions with Numbers	**4** **5**	Car Park (Selection of)	P
Unlimited Interchange **4** Limited Interchange **5**		Church	†
		City Wall	⊓⊓⊓⊓⊓
Primary Route	**A41**	Ferry (vehicular) ⛴ (foot only)	⛴
Dual Carriageways		Golf Course	⛳ ⛳
Class A Road	**A459**	Heliport	Ⓗ
Class B Road	**B5100**	Hospital	H
Major Roads Under Construction		Lighthouse	ⓘ
Major Roads Proposed		Market	⚏
Minor Roads		National Trust Property — (open) NT — (restricted opening) NT	
Fuel Station	⛽	(National Trust for Scotland) NTS NTS	
Restricted Access		Park & Ride	P+⊟⊟⊟
Pedestrianized Road & Main Footway		Place of Interest	▬ ▬ ■
One Way Streets	→ →	Police Station	▲
Toll	Toll	Post Office	★
Railway and Station	⊟	Shopping Area (Main street and precinct)	▯
Underground / Metro & D.L.R. Station	⊖ **DLR**	Shopmobility	🏍
Level Crossing and Tunnel	⊬ ⊟	Toilet	▽
Tram Stop and One Way Tram Stop	⊝ ⊝	Tourist Information Centre	𝒊
Built-up Area		Viewpoint	⛭ ⛭
		Visitor Information Centre	V

BIRMINGHAM

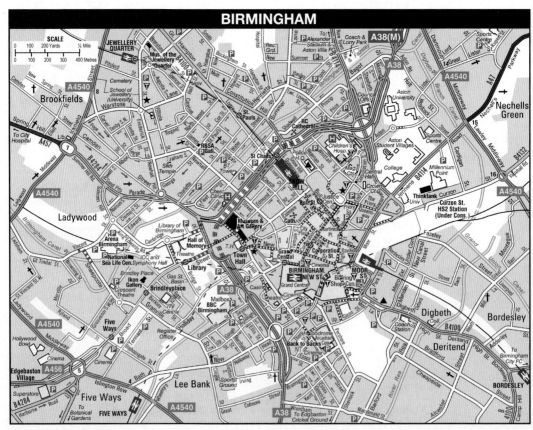

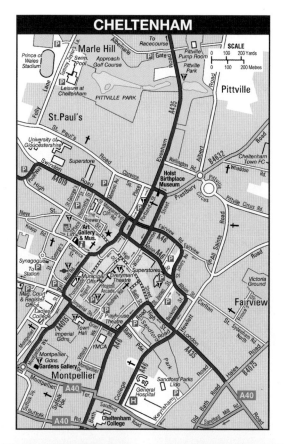

CHELTENHAM

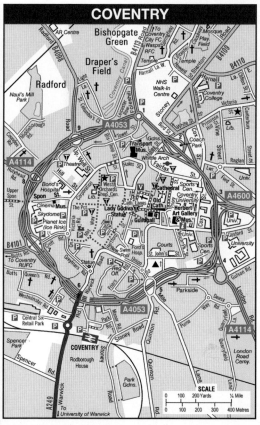

COVENTRY

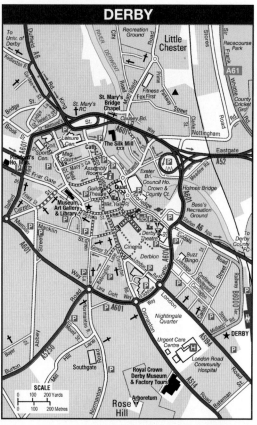

DERBY

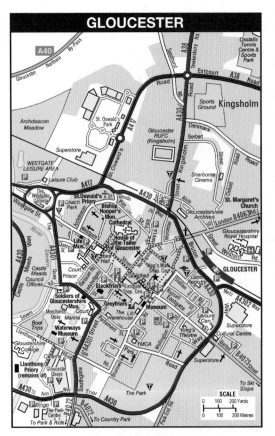

GLOUCESTER

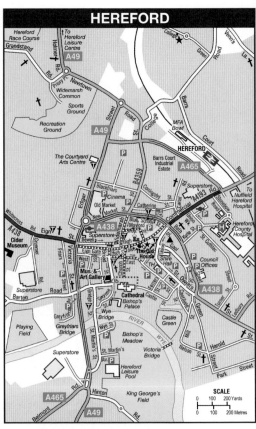

HEREFORD

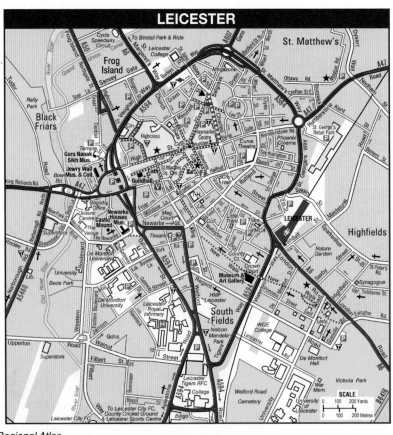

LEICESTER

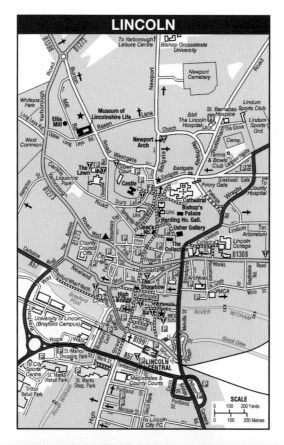

LINCOLN

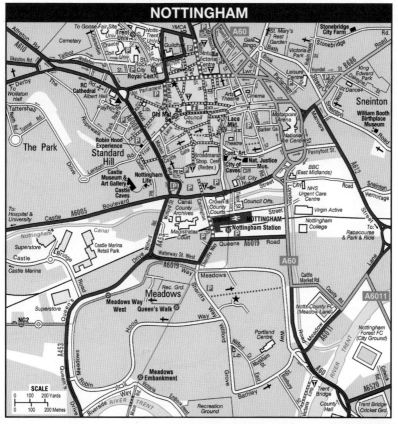

NOTTINGHAM

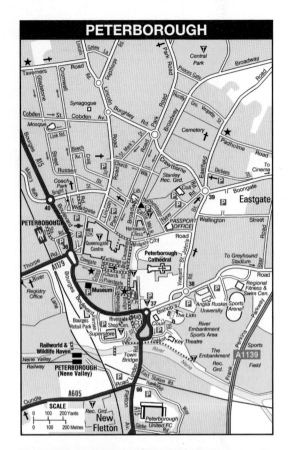

PETERBOROUGH

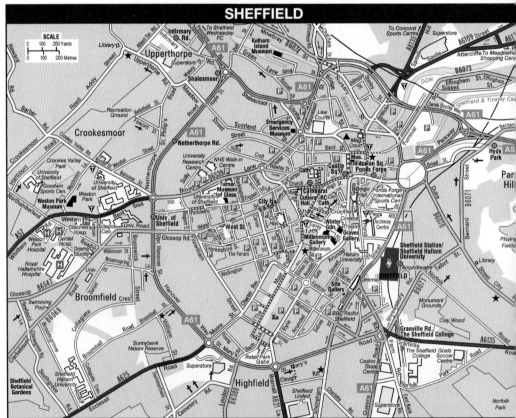

SHEFFIELD

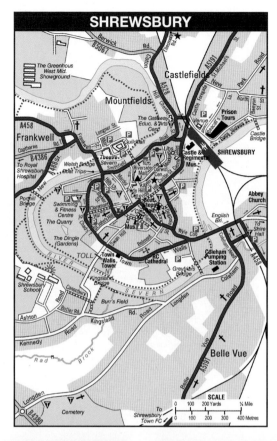

SHREWSBURY

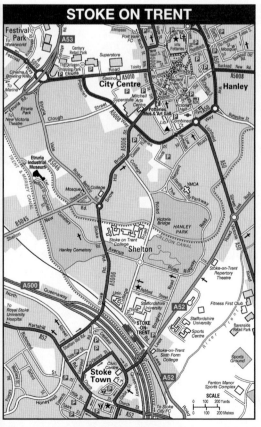

STOKE ON TRENT

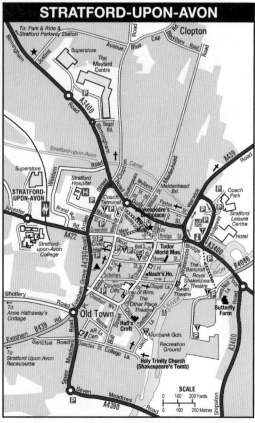

STRATFORD-UPON-AVON

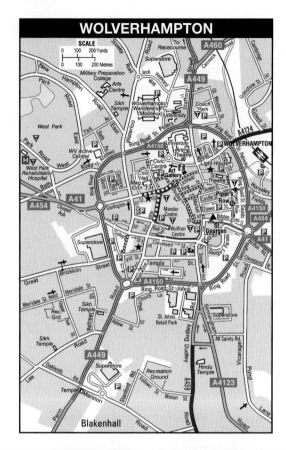

WOLVERHAMPTON

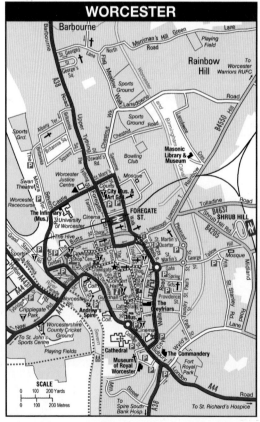

WORCESTER

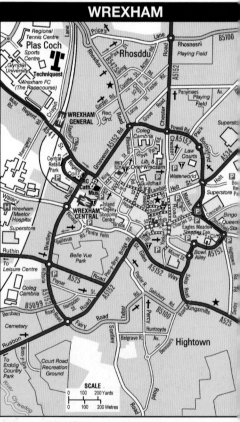

WREXHAM

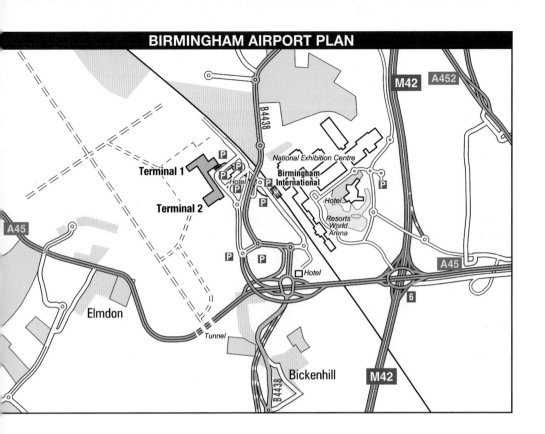

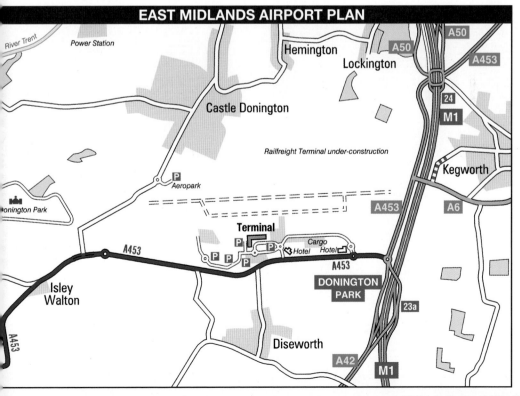

INDEX TO CITIES, TOWNS, VILLAGES, HAMLETS & LOCATIONS

1. A strict alphabetical order is used e.g. Westmancote follows West Malvern but precedes West Markham.
2. The map reference given refers to the actual map square in which the town spot or built-up area is located and not to the place name.
3. Only one reference is given although due to page overlaps the place may appear on more than one page.
4. Where two or more places of the same name occur in the same County or Unitary Authority, the nearest large town is also given; e.g. Blackwell *Derbs*.....2A **24** (nr Alfreton) indicates that Blackwell is located in square 2A on page **24** and is situated near Alfreton in the County of Derbyshire.
5. Major towns & destinations are shown in bold i.e. **Birmingham** *W Mid*.....**76** (3B **46**). Where they appear on a Town Plan a second page reference is given.

COUNTIES AND UNITARY AUTHORITIES with the abbreviations used in this index

Buckinghamshire : Buck
Cambridgeshire : *Cambs*
Cheshire East : *Ches E*
Cheshire West & Chester : *Ches W*
Denbighshire : *Den*
Derby : *Derb*
Derbyshire : *Derbs*
East Riding of Yorkshire : *E Yor*
Flintshire : *Flin*
Gloucestershire : *Glos*
Greater Manchester : *G Man*
Herefordshire : *Here*
Kingston upon Hull : *Hull*
Leicester : *Leic*
Leicestershire : *Leics*
Lincolnshire : *Linc*
Milton Keynes : *Mil*
Monmouthshire : *Mon*
Newport : *Newp*
Norfolk : *Norf*
North East Lincolnshire : *NE Lin*
North Lincolnshire : *N Lin*
North Yorkshire : *N Yor*
Northamptonshire : *Nptn*
Nottingham : *Nott*
Nottinghamshire : *Notts*
Oxfordshire : *Oxon*
Peterborough : *Pet*
Powys : *Powy*
Rutland : *Rut*
Shropshire : *Shrp*
South Gloucestershire : *S Glo*
South Yorkshire : *S Yor*
Staffordshire : *Staf*
Stoke-on-Trent : *Stoke*
Swindon : *Swin*
Telford & Wrekin : *Telf*
Torfaen : *Torf*
Warwickshire : *Warw*
West Midlands : *W Mid*
West Yorkshire : *W Yor*
Wiltshire : *Wilts*
Worcestershire : *Worc*
Wrexham : *Wrex*

INDEX

A

Abberley *Worc* 2B **56**
Abberley Common *Worc* 2B **56**
Abberton *Worc* 3D **57**
Abbeydale *S Yor* 2D **11**
Abbeydale Park *S Yor* 2D **11**
Abbey Dore *Here* 2B **62**
Abbey Hulton *Stoke* 3D **21**
Abbots Bromley *Staf* 2A **34**
Abbots Morton *Worc* 3A **58**
Abbot's Salford *Warw* 3A **58**
Abcott *Shrp* 1B **54**
Abdon *Shrp* 3A **44**
Abenhall *Glos* 1D **71**
Aberbechan *Powy* 2A **42**
Abergavenny *Mon* 1A **70**
Aber-miwl *Powy* 2A **42**
Abermule *Powy* 2A **42**
Aber-oer *Wrex* 3A **18**
Aberriw *Powy* 1A **42**
Abingdon-on-Thames *Oxon* 3D **75**
Ab Kettleby *Leics* 2D **37**
Ab Lench *Worc* 3A **58**
Ablington *Glos* 2A **74**
Abney *Derbs* 3B **10**
Abthorpe *Nptn* 1C **69**
Aby *Linc* 3C **17**
Achurch *Nptn* 3D **51**
Ackleton *Shrp* 2C **45**
Ackton *W Yor* 1B **4**
Ackworth Moor Top *W Yor* 2B **4**
Acocks Green *W Mid* 3C **47**
Aconbury *Here* 2D **63**
Acrefair *Wrex* 3A **18**
Acton *Ches E* 2A **20**
Acton *Shrp* 3C **43**
Acton *Staf* 3C **21**
Acton *Worc* 2C **57**
Acton *Wrex* 2B **18**
Acton Beauchamp *Here* 3A **56**
Acton Burnell *Shrp* 1A **44**
Acton Green *Here* 3A **56**
Acton Pigott *Shrp* 1A **44**
Acton Round *Shrp* 2B **44**
Acton Scott *Shrp* 3D **43**
Acton Trussell *Staf* 3D **33**
Adam's Hill *Worc* 1D **57**
Adbaston *Staf* 2B **32**
Adderbury *Oxon* 2A **68**
Adderley *Shrp* 1A **32**
Addington *Buck* 3D **69**
Addlethorpe *Linc* 1D **29**
Adeney *Telf* 3B **32**
Adforton *Here* 1C **55**
Adlestrop *Glos* 3C **67**
Adlingfleet *E Yor* 1B **6**
Admaston *Staf* 2A **34**
Admaston *Telf* 3A **32**
Admington *Warw* 1C **67**
Adstock *Buck* 2D **69**
Adstone *Nptn* 3B **60**
Adwick le Street *S Yor* 3C **5**
Adwick upon Dearne *S Yor* 3B **4**
Ailey *Here* 1B **62**
Ailsworth *Pet* 2A **52**
Airedale *W Yor* 1B **4**
Airmyn *E Yor* 1A **6**
Aisby *Linc* 1A **14**
(nr Gainsborough)
Aisby *Linc* 1C **39**
(nr Grantham)
Aisthorpe *Linc* 2B **14**
Akeley *Buck* 2D **69**
Alberbury *Shrp* 3B **30**
Albert Village *Leics* 3D **35**
Albrighton *Shrp* 3C **31**
(nr Shrewsbury)
Albrighton *Shrp* 1D **45**
(nr Telford)
Alcaston *Shrp* 3D **43**
Alcester *Warw* 3A **58**
Aldercar *Derbs* 3A **24**
Alderley *Glos* 3A **72**
Alderminster *Warw* 1C **67**
Alder Moor *Staf* 2C **35**
Aldersey Green *Ches W* 2C **19**
Alderton *Glos* 2A **66**
Alderton *Nptn* 1D **69**
Alderton *Shrp* 2C **31**
Alderton Fields *Glos* 2A **66**
Alderwasley *Derbs* 2D **23**
Aldford *Ches W* 2C **19**
Aldgate *Rut* 1C **51**
Aldington *Worc* 1A **66**
Aldon *Shrp* 1C **55**
Aldridge *W Mid* 1B **46**
Aldsworth *Glos* 1A **74**
Aldwark *Derbs* 2C **23**
Aldwincle *Nptn* 3D **51**
Alford *Linc* 3C **17**
Alfreton *Derbs* 2A **24**
Alfrick *Worc* 3B **56**
Alfrick Pound *Worc* 3B **56**
Algarkirk *Linc* 1A **40**
Alkborough *N Lin* 1B **6**
Alkerton *Oxon* 1D **67**
Alkington *Shrp* 1D **31**
Alkmonton *Derbs* 1B **34**
Allaston *Glos* 2D **71**
Allen End *Warw* 2C **47**
Allensmore *Here* 2C **63**
Allenton *Derb* 1D **35**
Allerton Bywater *W Yor* 1B **4**
Allesley *W Mid* 3D **47**
Allestree *Derb* 1D **35**
Allexton *Leics* 1B **50**
Allgreave *Ches E* 1D **21**
Allimore Green *Staf* 3C **33**
Allington *Linc* 3A **26**
Allscott *Shrp* 2C **45**
Allscott *Telf* 3A **32**
All Stretton *Shrp* 2D **43**
Alltami *Flin* 1A **18**
Almeley *Here* 3B **54**
Almeley Wootton *Here* 3B **54**
Almholme *S Yor* 3C **5**
Almington *Staf* 1B **32**
Alport *Derbs* 1C **23**
Alport *Powy* 2B **42**
Alpraham *Ches E* 2D **19**
Alrewas *Staf* 3B **34**
Alsager *Ches E* 2B **20**
Alsagers Bank *Staf* 3C **21**
Alsop en le Dale *Derbs* 2B **22**
Alstone *Glos* 2D **65**
Alstonefield *Staf* 2B **22**
Althorpe *N Lin* 3B **6**
Altofts *W Yor* 1A **4**
Alton *Derbs* 1D **23**
Alton *Staf* 3A **22**
Alvaston *Derb* 1D **35**
Alvechurch *Worc* 1A **58**
Alvecote *Warw* 1D **47**
Alveley *Shrp* 3C **45**
Alverthorpe *W Yor* 1A **4**
Alverton *Notts* 3D **25**
Alvescot *Oxon* 2B **74**
Alveston *Warw* 3C **59**
Alvingham *Linc* 1B **16**
Alvington *Glos* 2D **71**
Alwalton *Cambs* 2A **52**
Ambaston *Derbs* 1A **36**
Ambergate *Derbs* 2D **23**
Amber Hill *Linc* 3A **28**
Amberley *Glos* 2B **72**
Amblecote *W Mid* 3D **45**
Amcotts *N Lin* 2B **6**
Amerton *Staf* 2D **33**
Ampney Crucis *Glos* 2D **73**
Ampney St Mary *Glos* 2D **73**
Ampney St Peter *Glos* 2D **73**
Ancaster *Linc* 3B **26**
Anchor *Shrp* 3A **42**
Anderby *Linc* 3D **17**
Anderby Creek *Linc* 3D **17**
Andoversford *Glos* 1D **73**
Angelbank *Shrp* 1D **55**
Ankerbold *Derbs* 1D **23**
Anlaby *E Yor* 1D **7**
Anlaby Park *Hull* 1D **7**
Annesley *Notts* 2B **24**
Annesley Woodhouse *Notts* 2B **24**
Annscroft *Shrp* 1D **43**
Ansley *Warw* 2D **47**
Anslow *Staf* 2C **35**
Anslow Gate *Staf* 2B **34**
Anstey *Leics* 1C **49**
Ansty *Warw* 3A **48**
Anton's Gowt *Linc* 3A **28**
Anwick *Linc* 2D **27**
Apethorpe *Nptn* 2D **51**
Apeton *Staf* 3C **33**
Apley *Linc* 3D **15**
Apperknowle *Derbs* 3D **11**
Apperley *Glos* 3C **65**
Appleby *N Lin* 2C **7**
Appleby Magna *Leics* 1A **48**
Appleby Parva *Leics* 1A **48**
Appleton *Oxon* 2D **75**
Appletree *Nptn* 1A **68**
Arbourthorne *S Yor* 2D **11**
Arclid *Ches E* 1B **20**
Arclid Green *Ches E* 1B **20**
Arddleen *Powy* 3A **30**
Arddlîn *Powy* 3A **30**
Ardens Grafton *Warw* 3B **58**
Ardley *Oxon* 3B **68**
Ardsley *S Yor* 3A **4**
Areley Common *Worc* 1C **57**
Areley Kings *Worc* 1C **57**
Arksey *S Yor* 3C **5**
Arkwright Town *Derbs* 3A **12**
Arlescote *Warw* 1D **67**
Arleston *Telf* 3A **32**
Arlingham *Glos* 1A **72**
Arlington *Glos* 2A **74**
Armitage *Staf* 3A **34**
Armscote *Warw* 1C **67**
Armston *Nptn* 3D **51**
Armthorpe *S Yor* 3D **5**
Arnesby *Leics* 2D **49**
Arnold *Notts* 3B **24**
Arrow *Warw* 3A **58**
Arthingworth *Nptn* 3A **50**
Ascott-under-Wychwood *Oxon* 1C **75**
Asfordby *Leics* 3D **37**
Asfordby Hill *Leics* 3D **37**
Asgarby *Linc* 1B **28**
(nr Horncastle)
Asgarby *Linc* 3D **27**
(nr Sleaford)
Ashbourne *Derbs* 3B **22**
Ashbrook *Shrp* 2D **43**
Ashby *N Lin* 3B **6**
Ashby by Partney *Linc* 1C **29**
Ashby cum Fenby *NE Lin* 3B **8**
Ashby de la Launde *Linc* 2C **27**
Ashby-de-la-Zouch *Leics* 3D **35**
Ashby Folville *Leics* 3D **37**
Ashby Magna *Leics* 2C **49**
Ashby Parva *Leics* 3C **49**
Ashby Puerorum *Linc* 3B **16**
Ashby St Ledgers *Nptn* 2B **60**
Ashchurch *Glos* 2D **65**
Ashfield *Here* 3D **63**
Ashfield *Shrp* 3A **44**
Ashford Bowdler *Shrp* 1D **55**
Ashford Carbonel *Shrp* 1D **55**
Ashford in the Water *Derbs* 1B **22**
Ash Green *Warw* 3A **48**
Ashleworth *Glos* 3C **65**
Ashley *Glos* 3C **73**
Ashley *Nptn* 2A **50**
Ashley *Staf* 1B **32**
Ashley Heath *Staf* 1B **32**
Ashley Moor *Here* 2C **55**
Ash Magna *Shrp* 1D **31**
Ashmead Green *Glos* 3A **72**
Ashorne *Warw* 3D **59**
Ashover *Derbs* 1D **23**
Ashow *Warw* 1D **59**
Ash Parva *Shrp* 1D **31**
Ashperton *Here* 1A **64**
Ashton *Here* 2D **55**
Ashton *Nptn* 3D **51**
(nr Oundle)
Ashton *Nptn* 1D **69**
(nr Roade)
Ashton *Pet* 1A **52**
Ashton Hayes *Ches W* 1D **19**
Ashton Keynes *Wilts* 3D **73**
Ashton under Hill *Worc* 2D **65**
Ashwell *Rut* 3A **38**
Ashwood *Staf* 3D **45**
Askern *S Yor* 2C **5**
Askham *Notts* 3D **13**
Aslackby *Linc* 1C **39**
Aslockton *Notts* 3D **25**
Asperton *Linc* 1A **40**
Asselby *E Yor* 1A **6**
Astbury *Ches E* 1C **21**
Astcote *Nptn* 3C **61**
Asterby *Linc* 3A **16**
Asterley *Shrp* 1C **43**
Asterton *Shrp* 2C **43**
Asthall *Oxon* 1B **74**
Asthall Leigh *Oxon* 1C **75**
Astley *Shrp* 3D **31**
Astley *Warw* 3A **48**
Astley *Worc* 2B **56**
Astley Abbotts *Shrp* 2C **45**
Astley Cross *Worc* 2C **57**
Aston *Ches E* 3A **20**
Aston *Derbs* 2B **10**
(nr Hope)
Aston *Derbs* 1B **34**
(nr Sudbury)
Aston *Flin* 1B **18**
Aston *Here* 2C **55**
Aston *Oxon* 2C **75**
Aston *S Yor* 2A **12**
Aston *Shrp* 2D **45**
(nr Bridgnorth)
Aston *Shrp* 2D **31**
(nr Wem)
Aston *Staf* 3B **20**
Aston *Telf* 1B **44**
Aston *W Mid* 2B **46**
Aston Botterell *Shrp* 3B **44**
Aston-by-Stone *Staf* 1D **33**
Aston Cantlow *Warw* 3B **58**
Aston Crews *Here* 3A **64**
Aston Cross *Glos* 2D **65**
Aston Eyre *Shrp* 2B **44**
Aston Fields *Worc* 2D **57**
Aston Flamville *Leics* 2B **48**
Aston Ingham *Here* 3A **64**
Aston juxta Mondrum *Ches E* 2A **20**
Astonlane *Shrp* 2B **44**
Aston le Walls *Nptn* 3A **60**
Aston Magna *Glos* 2B **66**
Aston Munslow *Shrp* 3A **44**
Aston on Carrant *Glos* 2D **65**
Aston on Clun *Shrp* 3C **43**
Aston-on-Trent *Derbs* 2A **36**
Aston Pigott *Shrp* 1C **43**
Aston Rogers *Shrp* 1C **43**
Aston Somerville *Worc* 2A **66**
Aston Subedge *Glos* 1B **66**
Astrop *Nptn* 2B **68**
Astwood Bank *Worc* 2A **58**
Aswarby *Linc* 1C **39**
Aswardby *Linc* 3B **16**
Atcham *Shrp* 1A **44**
Atch Lench *Worc* 3A **58**
Athersley *S Yor* 3A **4**
Atherstone *Warw* 2A **48**
Atherstone on Stour *Warw* 3C **59**
Atlow *Derbs* 3C **23**
Attenborough *Notts* 1B **36**
Atterby *Linc* 1B **14**
Atterley *Shrp* 2B **44**
Atterton *Leics* 2A **48**
Attleborough *Warw* 2A **48**
Auberrow *Here* 1C **63**
Aubourn *Linc* 1B **26**
Auckley *S Yor* 3D **5**
Audlem *Ches E* 3A **20**
Audley *Staf* 2B **20**
Audmore *Staf* 2C **33**
Aughton *S Yor* 2A **12**
Aulden *Here* 3C **55**
Ault Hucknall *Derbs* 1A **24**
Aunby *Linc* 3C **39**
Aunsby *Linc* 1C **39**
Austerfield *S Yor* 1C **13**
Austin Fen *Linc* 1B **16**
Austrey *Warw* 1D **47**
Authorpe *Linc* 2C **17**
Authorpe Row *Linc* 3D **17**
Avening *Glos* 3B **72**
Averham *Notts* 2D **25**
Avon Dassett *Warw* 3A **60**
Awre *Glos* 2A **72**
Awsworth *Notts* 3A **24**
Aylburton *Glos* 2D **71**
Aylburton Common *Glos* 2D **71**
Aylesby *NE Lin* 3B **8**
Aylestone *Leic* 1C **49**
Aylton *Here* 2A **64**
Aylworth *Glos* 3B **66**
Aymestrey *Here* 2C **55**
Aynho *Nptn* 2B **68**
Ayston *Rut* 1B **50**

B

Babbinswood *Shrp* 1B **30**
Bablock Hythe *Oxon* 2D **75**
Babworth *Notts* 2C **13**
Bacheldre *Powy* 2B **42**
Bacton *Here* 2B **62**
Badby *Nptn* 3B **60**
Baddeley Green *Stoke* 2D **21**
Baddesley Clinton *W Mid* 1C **59**
Baddesley Ensor *Warw* 2D **47**
Badgeworth *Glos* 1C **73**
Badsey *Worc* 1A **66**
Badsworth *W Yor* 2B **4**
Bag Enderby *Linc* 3B **16**
Bagendon *Glos* 2D **73**
Bagginswood *Shrp* 3B **44**
Baginton *Warw* 1D **59**
Bagley *Shrp* 2C **31**
Bagnall *Staf* 2D **21**
Bagthorpe *Notts* 2A **24**
Bagworth *Leics* 1B **48**
Bagwyllydiart *Here* 3C **63**
Bainton *Oxon* 3B **68**
Bainton *Pet* 1D **51**
Bakewell *Derbs* 1C **23**
Balby *S Yor* 3
Balderton *Ches W* 1B
Balderton *Notts* 2A
Baldwin's Gate *Staf* 1B
Balkholme *E Yor* 1
Ball *Shrp* 2B
Ballidon *Derbs* 2C
Ballingham *Here* 2D
Balsall *W Mid* 1C
Balsall Common *W Mid* 1C
Balscote *Oxon* 1D
Balterley *Staf* 2B
Bamford *Derbs* 2C
Bampton *Oxon* 2C
Banbury *Oxon* 1A
Bangor-is-y-coed *Wrex* 3B
Bank, The *Ches E* 2C
Bank, The *Shrp* 2B
Bank Street *Worc* 2A
Banners Gate *W Mid* 2B
Barber Booth *Derbs* 2B
Barbourne *Worc* 3C
Barbridge *Ches E* 2A
Barby *Nptn* 1B
Barby Nortoft *Nptn* 1B
Barcheston *Warw* 2C
Bardney *Linc* 1D
Bardon *Leics* 3A
Barford *Warw* 2C
Barford St John *Oxon* 2A
Barford St Michael *Oxon* 2A
Barholm *Linc* 3C
Barkby *Leics* 1D
Barkestone-le-Vale *Leics* 1D
Barkston *Linc* 3B
Barlaston *Staf* 1C
Barlborough *Derbs* 3A
Barlestone *Leics* 1B
Barleythorpe *Rut* 1B
Barlings *Linc* 3C
Barlow *Derbs* 3D
Barlow *N Yor* 1
Barmby on the Marsh *E Yor* 1
Barnack *Pet* 1D
Barnacle *Warw* 3A
Barnard Gate *Oxon* 1D
Barnburgh *S Yor* 3
Barnby Dun *S Yor* 3
Barnby in the Willows *Notts* 2A
Barnby Moor *Notts* 2C
Barnetby le Wold *N Lin* 3
Barnoldby le Beck *NE Lin* 3
Barnsley *Glos* 2D
Barnsley *S Yor*
Barnsley *Shrp* 2C
Barnstone *Notts* 1D
Barnt Green *Worc* 1A
Barnwell *Nptn* 3D
Barnwood *Glos* 1B
Barons Cross *Here* 3C
Barrow *Rut* 3A
Barrow *Shrp* 1B
Barrowby *Linc* 1A
Barrowden *Rut* 1C
Barrow Haven *N Lin* 1
Barrow Hill *Derbs* 3A
Barrow upon Humber *N Lin* 1
Barrow upon Soar *Leics* 3B
Barrow upon Trent *Derbs* 2D
Barsby *Leics* 3C
Barston *W Mid* 1C
Bartestree *Here* 1D
Barthomley *Ches E* 2B
Bartley Green *W Mid* 3B
Barton *Ches W* 2C
Barton *Glos* 3B
Barton *Warw* 3B
Barton Gate *Staf* 3B
Barton Green *Staf* 3B
Barton Hartshorn *Buck* 2C
Barton in Fabis *Notts* 1B
Barton in the Beans *Leics* 1A
Barton-on-the-Heath *Warw* 2C
Barton-Under-Needwood *Staf* 3B
Barton-upon-Humber *N Lin* 1
Barton Waterside *N Lin* 1
Barugh Green *S Yor* 3
Barwell *Leics* 2B
Baschurch *Shrp* 2C
Bascote *Warw* 2A
Basford Green *Staf* 2D
Baslow *Derbs* 3C
Bassingfield *Notts* 1C
Bassingham *Linc* 1B
Bassingthorpe *Linc* 2B
Baston *Linc* 3D
Bastonford *Worc* 3C
Batchley *Worc* 2A

Burntwood Green – Crackley

Burntwood Green Staf 1B 46
Burringham N Lin 3B 6
Burrington Here 1C 55
Burrough on the Hill Leics 3D 37
Burslem Stoke 3C 21
Burston Staf 1D 33
Burstwick E Yor 1B 8
Burtoft Linc 1A 40
Burton Ches W 1D 19
Burton Wrex 2B 18
Burton-by-Lincoln Linc 3B 14
Burton Coggles Linc 2B 38
Burton Corner Linc 3B 28
Burton Green Warw 1C 59
Burton Green Wrex 2B 18
Burton Hastings Warw 3B 48
Burton Joyce Notts 3C 25
Burton Lazars Leics 3D 37
Burton on the Wolds Leics 2B 36
Burton Overy Leics 2D 49
Burton Pedwardine Linc 3D 27
Burton Salmon N Yor 1B 4
Burton Stather N Lin 2B 6
Burton upon Stather N Lin 2B 6
Burton upon Trent Staf 2C 35
Burton Wolds Leics 2C 37
Burwardsley Ches W 2D 19
Burwarton Shrp 3B 44
Burwell Linc 3B 16
Bury Cambs 3B 52
Burybank Staf 1C 33
Bury End Worc 2A 66
Buscot Oxon 3B 74
Bush Bank Here 3C 55
Bushbury W Mid 1A 46
Bushby Leics 1D 49
Bushley Worc 2C 65
Bushley Green Worc 2C 65
Bushmoor Shrp 3D 43
Buslingthorpe Linc 2C 15
Bussage Glos 2B 72
Butlers Marston Warw 1D 67
Butterton Staf 2A 22
(nr Leek)
Butterton Staf 3C 21
(nr Stoke-on-Trent)
Butterwick Linc 3B 28
Butt Green Ches E 2A 20
Buttington Powy 1B 42
Buttonbridge Shrp 1B 56
Buttonoak Shrp 1B 56
Buxton Derbs 3A 10
Buxworth Derbs 2A 10
Bwcle Flin 1A 18
Bwlchgwyn Wrex 2A 18
Byfield Nptn 3B 60
Byford Here 1B 62
Byley Ches W 1B 20
Byram N Yor 1B 4
Byton Here 2B 54

C

Cabourne Linc 3A 8
Cadeby Leics 1B 48
Cadeby S Yor 3C 5
Cadney N Lin 3D 7
Cadole Flin 1A 18
Caenby Linc 2C 15
Caergwrle Flin 2B 18
Caerleon Newp 3A 70
Caerllion Newp 3A 70
Caer-went Mon 3B 70
Caistor Linc 3A 8
Cakebole Worc 1C 57
Calceby Linc 3B 16
Calcot Glos 1D 73
Calcott Shrp 3C 31
Caldecote Cambs 3A 52
Caldecote Nptn 3C 61
Caldecote Warw 2A 48
Caldecott Oxon 3D 75
Caldecott Rut 2B 50
Calder Grove W Yor 2A 4
Caldwell Derbs 3C 35
Calf Heath Staf 1A 46
Calke Derbs 2D 35
Callaughton Shrp 2B 44
Callingwood Staf 2B 34
Callow Here 2C 63
Callowell Glos 2B 72
Callow End Worc 1C 65
Callow Hill Worc 1B 56
(nr Bewdley)
Callow Hill Worc 2A 58
(nr Redditch)
Calmsden Glos 2D 73
Calow Derbs 3A 12
Calton Staf 2B 22
Calveley Ches E 2D 19
Calver Derbs 3C 11
Calverhall Shrp 1A 32
Calvert Buck 3C 69
Calverton Mil 2D 69
Calverton Notts 3C 25
Cam Glos 3A 72
Camblesforth N Yor 1D 5
Cambridge Glos 2A 72
Camer's Green Worc 2B 64
Camerton E Yor 1B 8
Cammeringham Linc 2B 14
Camp, The Glos 2C 73
Campsall S Yor 2C 5
Candlesby Linc 1C 29
Canholes Derbs 3A 10
Canley W Mid 1D 59
Cannock Staf 3D 33
Cannock Wood Staf 3A 34
Canon Bridge Here 1C 63
Canon Frome Here 1A 64
Canon Pyon Here 1C 63
Canons Ashby Nptn 3B 60
Cantley S Yor 3D 5
Cantlop Shrp 1A 44
Canwick Linc 1B 26
Capel-y-ffin Powy 2A 62
Carbrook S Yor 2D 11
Carburton Notts 3C 13
Car Colston Notts 3D 25
Carcroft S Yor 3C 5
Cardeston Shrp 3B 30
Cardington Shrp 2A 44
Careby Linc 3C 39
Carey Here 2D 63
Carlby Linc 3C 39
Carleton W Yor 1B 4
Carlton Leics 1A 48
Carlton N Yor 1D 5
Carlton Notts 3C 25
Carlton S Yor 2A 4
Carlton W Yor 1A 4
Carlton Curlieu Leics 2D 49
Carlton in Lindrick Notts 2B 12
Carlton-le-Moorland Linc 2B 26
Carlton-on-Trent Notts 1A 26
Carlton Scroop Linc 3B 26
Carol Green W Mid 1C 59
Carrhouse N Lin 3A 6
Carrington Linc 2B 28
Carrow Hill Mon 3B 70
Carr Vale Derbs 1A 24
Carsington Derbs 2C 23
Carterton Oxon 2B 74
Cascob Powy 2A 54
Cas-gwent Mon 3C 71
Cassington Oxon 1D 75
Castle Bromwich W Mid 3C 47
Castle Bytham Linc 3B 38
Castle Caereinion Powy 1A 42
Castle Donington Leics 2A 36
Castle Eaton Swin 3A 74
Castleford W Yor 1B 4
Castle Frome Here 1A 64
Castle Green Warw 1C 59
Castle Gresley Derbs 3C 35
Castlemorton Worc 2B 64
Castlethorpe Mil 1D 69
Castleton Derbs 2B 10
Castor Pet 2A 52
Catbrook Mon 2D 71
Catchems End Worc 1B 56
Catcliffe S Yor 2A 12
Catherine-de-Barnes W Mid 3C 47
Catherton Shrp 1A 56
Cat's Ash Newp 3A 70
Catshill Worc 1D 57
Catthorpe Leics 1B 60
Caudle Green Glos 1C 73
Caulcott Oxon 3B 68
Cauldon Staf 3A 22
Cauldon Lowe Staf 3A 22
Caunsall Worc 3D 45
Caunton Notts 1D 25
Cavendish Bridge Leics 2A 36
Caversfield Oxon 3B 68
Caverswall Staf 3D 21
Cawkwell Linc 2A 16
Cawston Warw 1A 60
Cawthorpe Linc 2C 39
Caynham Shrp 1D 55
Caythorpe Linc 3B 26
Caythorpe Notts 3C 25
Cefn Canol Powy 1A 30
Cefn Einion Shrp 3B 42
Cefn-mawr Wrex 3A 18
Cefn-y-bedd Flin 2B 18
Cefn-y-coed Powy 2A 42
Cegidfa Powy 3A 30
Cellarhead Staf 3D 21
Ceri Powy 3A 42
Cerney Wick Glos 3D 73
Chaceley Glos 2C 65
Chackmore Buck 2C 69
Chacombe Nptn 1A 68
Chaddesden Derb 1D 35
Chaddesden Common Derb 1D 35
Chaddesley Corbett Worc 1C 57
Chadlington Oxon 3D 67
Chadshunt Warw 3D 59
Chad Valley W Mid 3B 46
Chadwell Leics 2D 37
Chadwell Shrp 3B 32
Chadwick End W Mid 1C 59
Chain Bridge Linc 3B 28
Chainbridge Cambs 1D 53
Chalford Glos 2B 72
Chalk Hill Glos 3B 66
Chandler's Cross Worc 2B 64
Chapel Brampton Nptn 2D 61
Chapelbridge Cambs 2B 52
Chapel Chorlton Staf 1C 33
Chapel-en-le-Frith Derbs 2A 10
Chapelgate Linc 2C 41
Chapel Green Warw 3B 60
(nr Coventry)
Chapel Green Warw 2A 60
(nr Southam)
Chapel Haddlesey N Yor 1C 5
Chapel Hill Linc 2A 28
Chapel Hill Mon 2C 71
Chapel Lawn Shrp 1B 54
Chapel Milton Derbs 2A 10
Chapel St Leonards Linc 3D 17
Chapelthorpe W Yor 2A 4
Chapeltown S Yor 1D 11
Charfield S Glo 3A 72
Charingworth Glos 2C 67
Charlbury Oxon 1C 75
Charlecote Warw 3C 59
Charlesworth Derbs 1A 10
Charlton Nptn 2B 68
Charlton Telf 3D 31
Charlton Worc 1A 66
(nr Evesham)
Charlton Worc 1C 57
(nr Stourport-on-Severn)
Charlton Abbots Glos 3A 66
Charlton Kings Glos 3D 65
Charndon Buck 3C 69
Charney Bassett Oxon 3C 75
Charterville Allotments Oxon 1C 75
Charwelton Nptn 3B 60
Chase Terrace Staf 1B 46
Chasetown Staf 1B 46
Chastleton Oxon 3C 67
Chatcull Staf 1B 32
Chatley Worc 2C 57
Chatteris Cambs 3C 53
Chatwall Shrp 2A 44
Chawley Oxon 2D 75
Chaxhill Glos 1A 72
Cheadle Staf 3A 22
Chebsey Staf 2C 33
Checkley Ches E 3B 20
Checkley Here 2D 63
Checkley Staf 1A 34
Cheddleton Staf 2D 21
Chedglow Wilts 3C 73
Chedworth Glos 1D 73
Chellaston Derb 1D 35
Chelmarsh Shrp 3C 45
Chelmick Shrp 2D 43
Chelmorton Derbs 1B 22
Cheltenham Glos 77 (3D 65)
Chelworth Wilts 3C 73
Chelworth Lower Green Wilts 3D 73
Chelworth Upper Green Wilts 3D 73
Cheney Longville Shrp 3D 43
Chepstow Mon 3C 71
Chequerfield W Yor 1B 4
Chequers Corner Norf 1D 53
Cherington Glos 3C 73
Cherington Warw 2C 67
Cherrington Telf 2A 32
Cherry Willingham Linc 3C 15
Cheslyn Hay Staf 1A 46
Chessetts Wood Warw 1B 58
Chester Ches W 1C 19
Chesterfield Derbs 3D 11
Chesterfield Staf 1C 47
Chesterton Cambs 2A 52
Chesterton Glos 2D 73
Chesterton Oxon 3B 68
Chesterton Shrp 2C 45
Chesterton Staf 3C 21
Chesterton Green Warw 3D 59
Cheswardine Shrp 1B 32
Cheswell Telf 3B 32
Cheswick Green W Mid 1B 58
Chetton Shrp 2B 44
Chetwode Buck 3C 69
Chetwynd Aston Telf 3B 32
Chickward Here 3A 54
Chilcote Leics 3C 35
Child's Ercall Shrp 2A 32
Childswickham Worc 2A 66
Chilson Oxon 1C 75
Chilwell Notts 1B 36
Chimney Oxon 2C 75
Chinley Derbs 2A 10
Chipnall Shrp 1B 32
Chipping Campden Glos 2B 66
Chipping Norton Oxon 3D 67
Chipping Warden Nptn 1A 68
Chirbury Shrp 2B 42
Chirk Wrex 1A 30
Cholstrey Here 3C 55
Chorley Ches E 2D 19
Chorley Shrp 3B 44
Chorley Staf 3A 34
Chorlton Ches E 2B 20
Chorlton Lane Ches W 3C 19
Choulton Shrp 3C 43
Christchurch Cambs 2D 53
Christchurch Glos 1C 71
Christleton Ches W 1C 19
Chunal Derbs 1A 10
Churcham Glos 1A 72
Church Aston Telf 3B 32
Church Brampton Nptn 2D 61
Church Broughton Derbs 1C 35
Churchdown Glos 3C 65
Church Eaton Staf 3C 33
Church End Cambs 3B 52
(nr Sawtry)
Church End Cambs 1C 53
(nr Wisbech)
Church End Glos 2A 72
Church End Linc 1A 40
(nr Donington)
Church End Linc 1C 17
(nr North Somercotes)
Church End Norf 3D 41
Church End Warw 2D 47
(nr Coleshill)
Church End Warw 2D 47
(nr Nuneaton)
Church Enstone Oxon 3D 67
Church Gresley Derbs 3C 35
Church Hanborough Oxon 1D 75
Church Hill Ches W 1A 20
Church Hill Worc 2A 58
Churchill Oxon 3C 67
Churchill Worc 1C 57
(nr Kidderminster)
Churchill Worc 3D 57
(nr Worcester)
Church Laneham Notts 3A 14
Church Langton Leics 2A 50
Church Lawford Warw 1A 60
Church Lawton Ches E 2C 21
Church Leigh Staf 1A 34
Church Lench Worc 3A 58
Church Mayfield Staf 3B 22
Church Minshull Ches E 1A 20
Churchover Warw 3C 49
Church Preen Shrp 2A 44
Church Pulverbatch Shrp 1D 43
Church Stoke Powy 2B 42
Church Stowe Nptn 3C 61
Church Stretton Shrp 2D 43
Church Town Leics 3D 35
Church Town N Lin 3A 6
Churchtown Derbs 1C 23
Churchtown Shrp 3B 42
Church Warsop Notts 1B 24
Church Westcote Glos 3C 67
Church Wilne Derbs 1A 36
Churton Ches W 2C 19
Cinderford Glos 1D 71
Cinderhill Derbs 3D 23
Cirencester Glos 2D 73
City Powy 2B 42
City Centre Stoke 3C 21
Cladswell Worc 3A 58
Clanfield Oxon 2B 74
Clapton-on-the-Hill Glos 1A 74
Clarborough Notts 2D 13
Clark's Hill Linc 2B 40
Claverdon Warw 2B 58
Claverley Shrp 2C 45
Clawson Hill Leics 2D 37
Claxby Linc 3C 17
(nr Alford)
Claxby Linc 1D 15
(nr Market Rasen)
Claybrooke Magna Leics 3B 48
Claybrooke Parva Leics 3B 48
Clay Coton Nptn 1B 60
Clay Cross Derbs 1D 23
Claydon Oxon 3A 60
Clayhanger W Mid 1B 46
Clay Lake Linc 2A 40
Claypits Glos 2A 72
Claypole Linc 3A 26
Claythorpe Linc 3C 17
Clayton S Yor 3B 4
Clayton Staf 3C 21
Clayworth Notts 2D 13
Clearwell Glos 2C 71
Cleedownton Shrp 3A 44
Cleehill Shrp 1D 55
Clee St Margaret Shrp 3A 44
Cleestanton Shrp 1D 55
Cleethorpes NE Lin 3C 9
Cleeton St Mary Shrp 1A 56
Cleeve Hill Glos 3D 65
Cleeve Prior Worc 1A 66
Clehonger Here 2C 63
Clenchwarton Norf 2D 41
Clent Worc 1D 57
Cleobury Mortimer Shrp 1A 56
Cleobury North Shrp 3B 44
Cleveley Oxon 3D 67
Clevelode Worc 1C 65
Cliff Warw 2D 47
Clifford Here 1A 62
Clifford Chambers Warw 3B 58
Clifford's Mesne Glos 3B 64
Clifton Derbs 3B 22
Clifton Nott 1B 36
Clifton Oxon 2A 68
Clifton S Yor 1B 12
Clifton Worc 1C 65
Clifton Campville Staf 3C 35
Clifton Hill Worc 2B 56
Clifton upon Dunsmore Warw 1B 60
Clifton upon Teme Worc 2B 56
Clipsham Rut 3B 38
Clipston Notts 1C 37
Clipston Nptn 3A 50
Clipstone Notts 1B 24
Clive Shrp 2D 31
Clixby Linc 3D 7
Cloddiau Powy 1B 42
Clodock Here 3B 62
Clopton Nptn 3D 51
Clotton Ches W 1D 19
Clowne Derbs 3A 12
Clows Top Worc 1B 56
Cloy Wrex 3B 18
Cluddley Telf 3A 32
Clun Shrp 3C 43
Clunbury Shrp 3C 43
Clungunford Shrp 1B 54
Clunton Shrp 3C 43
Clutton Ches W 2C 19
Clyro Powy 1A 62
Coal Aston Derbs 3D 11
Coalbrookdale Telf 1B 44
Coaley Glos 2A 72
Coal Pool W Mid 1B 46
Coalport Telf 1C 45
Coalville Leics 3A 36
Coalway Glos 1C 71
Coates Cambs 2C 53
Coates Glos 2C 73
Coates Linc 2B 14
Coberley Glos 1C 73
Cobhall Common Here 2C 63
Cobnash Here 2C 55
Cock Bank Wrex 3B 18
Cock Gate Here 2C 55
Cockshutford Shrp 3A 44
Cockshutt Shrp 2C 31
Cockyard Derbs 3A 10
Cockyard Here 2C 63
Coddington Ches W 2C 19
Coddington Here 1B 64
Coddington Notts 2A 26
Codnor Derbs 3A 24
Codsall Staf 1D 45
Codsall Wood Staf 1D 45
Coed Morgan Mon 1A 70
Coedpoeth Wrex 2A 18
Coedway Powy 3B 30
Coed-y-paen Mon 3A 70
Cofton Hackett Worc 1A 58
Cogges Oxon 2C 75
Cokhay Green Derbs 2C 35
Cold Ashby Nptn 1C 61
Cold Aston Glos 1A 74
Coldham Cambs 1D 53
Coldham Staf 1D 45
Cold Hanworth Linc 2C 15
Coldharbour Glos 2C 71
Cold Hatton Telf 2A 32
Cold Hatton Heath Telf 2A 32
Cold Hiendley W Yor 2A 4
Cold Higham Nptn 3C 61
Coldmeece Staf 1C 33
Cold Overton Leics 3A 38
Coldwell Here 2C 63
Colebatch Shrp 3C 43
Coleby Linc 1B 26
Coleby N Lin 2B 6
Cole End Warw 3D 47
Coleford Glos 1C 71
Colemere Shrp 1C 31
Colemore Green Shrp 2C 45
Coleorton Leics 3A 36
Colesbourne Glos 1D 73
Coles Green Worc 3B 56
Coleshill Oxon 3B 74
Coleshill Warw 3D 47
Colethrop Glos 1B 72
Collingham Notts 1A 26
Collingtree Nptn 3D 61
Collins Green Worc 3B 56
Collyweston Nptn 1C
Coln Rogers Glos 2D
Coln St Aldwyns Glos 2A
Coln St Dennis Glos 1D
Colsterworth Linc 2B
Colston Bassett Notts 1D
Colton Staf 2A
Colwall Here 1B
Colwall Green Here 1B
Colwich Staf 2A
Colwick Notts 3C
Combe Here 2B
Combe Oxon 1D
Combe Moor Here 2B
Comberford Staf 1C
Comberton Here 2C
Combridge Staf 1A
Combrook Warw 3D
Combs Derbs 3A
Comhampton Worc 2C
Comley Shrp 2D
Common Hill Here 2D
Common Side Derbs 3D
Commonside Derbs 3C
Compton Staf 3D
Compton Abdale Glos 1D
Conderton Worc 2D
Condicote Glos 3B
Condover Shrp 1D
Congerstone Leics 1A
Congleton Ches E 1C
Congreve Staf 3D
Coningsby Linc 2A
Conington Cambs 3A
Conisbrough S Yor 1B
Conisholme Linc 1C
Consall Staf 3D
Cookhill Worc 3A
Cookley Worc 3D
Cooksey Green Worc 2D
Cookshill Staf 3D
Coombe Glos 3A
Coombe Hill Glos 3C
Copalder Corner Cambs 2C
Coplow Dale Derbs 3B
Coppenhall Ches E 2B
Coppenhall Staf 3D
Coppenhall Moss Ches E 2B
Coppicegate Shrp 3C
Coppingford Cambs 3A
Copston Magna Warw 3B
Copt Green Warw 2B
Copt Heath W Mid 1B
Coptiviney Shrp 1C
Corby Nptn 3B
Corby Glen Linc 2B
Coreley Shrp 1A
Corfton Shrp 3D
Corley Warw 3A
Corley Ash Warw 3D
Corley Moor Warw 3D
Cornwell Oxon 3C
Corringham Linc 1A
Corse Glos 3B
Corse Lawn Worc 2C
Cosby Leics 2C
Coseley W Mid 2A
Cosgrove Nptn 1D
Coskills N Lin 2D
Cossall Notts 3A
Cossington Leics 3C
Costock Notts 2B
Coston Leics 2A
Cote Oxon 2C
Cotebrook Ches W 1D
Cotes Leics 2B
Cotes Staf 1C
Cotesbach Leics 3C
Cotes Heath Staf 1C
Cotgrave Notts 1C
Cotham Notts 3D
Cotheridge Worc 3B
Cothill Oxon 3D
Cotland Mon 2C
Cotmanhay Derbs 3A
Coton Nptn 1C
Coton Staf 2C
(nr Gnosa
Coton Staf 1D
(nr Stor
Coton Staf 1C
(nr Tamwor
Coton Clanford Staf 2C
Coton Hayes Staf 1D
Coton Hill Shrp 3C
Coton in the Clay Staf 2B
Coton in the Elms Derbs 3C
Cotonwood Shrp 1D
Cotonwood Staf 2C
Cottam Notts 3A
Cottarville Nptn 2D
Cotterstock Nptn 2D
Cottesbrooke Nptn 1D
Cottesmore Rut 3B
Cottingham Nptn 2B
Cottisford Oxon 2B
Cotton Staf 3A
Cotwalton Staf 1D
Coughton Here 3D
Coughton Warw 2A
Cound Shrp 1A
Countesthorpe Leics 2C
Courteenhall Nptn 3D
Coven Staf 1A
Coveney Cambs 3D
Covenham St Bartholomew Linc 1B
Covenham St Mary Linc 1B
Coven Heath Staf 1A
Coventry W Mid 77 (1D
Cowbit Linc 3A
Cowers Lane Derbs 3D
Cowley Glos 1C
Cowley Staf 3C
Coxall Here 1B
Coxbank Ches E 3A
Coxbench Derbs 3D
Coxgreen Staf 3D
Crabbs Cross Worc 2A
Crabtree Green Wrex 3B
Crackley Staf 2C

Crackley – Farnsfield

Crackley Warw 1C 59
Crackleybank Shrp 3B 32
Cradley Here 1B 64
Cradley W Mid 3A 46
Craig-llwyn Shrp 2A 30
Craignant Shrp 1A 30
Crakemarsh Staf 1A 34
Cranage Ches E 1B 20
Cranberry Staf 1C 33
Crane Moor S Yor 3A 4
Cranham Glos 1B 72
Cranmore Linc 1A 52
Cranoe Leics 2A 50
Cranwell Linc 3C 27
Craswall Here 2A 62
Craven Arms Shrp 3D 43
Crawley Oxon 1C 75
Creamore Bank Shrp 1D 31
Creaton Nptn 1D 61
Credenhill Here 1C 63
Creeton Linc 2C 39
Creighton Staf 1A 34
Cressage Shrp 1A 44
Cressbrook Derbs 3B 10
Cresswell Staf 1D 33
Creswell Derbs 3B 12
Creswell Green Staf 3A 34
Crewe Ches E 2B 20
Crewe-by-Farndon Ches W 2C 19
Crew Green Powy 3B 30
Crewton Derb 1D 35
Crich Derbs 2D 23
Crick Mon 3B 70
Crick Nptn 1B 60
Crickheath Shrp 2A 30
Cricklade Wilts 3A 74
Cridling Stubbs N Yor 1C 5
Criftins Shrp 1B 30
Criggion Powy 3A 30
Crigglestone W Yor 2A 4
Crimscote Warw 1C 67
Crocker's Ash Here 1C 71
Croes-hywel Mon 1A 70
Croesoswallt Shrp 2A 30
Croesyceiliog Torf 3A 70
Croesymwyalch Torf 3A 70
Croft Leics 2C 49
Croft Linc 1D 29
Crofton W Yor 2A 4
Cromford Derbs 2C 23
Cromhall S Glo 3D 71
Cromwell Notts 1D 25
Crookes S Yor 2D 11
Cropredy Oxon 1A 68
Cropston Leics 3B 36
Cropthorne Worc 1D 65
Cropwell Bishop Notts 1C 37
Cropwell Butler Notts 1C 37
Crosby N Lin 2B 6
Cross Ash Mon 1B 70
Crossgate Staf 1D 33
Cross Green Staf 1A 46
Cross Hill Derbs 3A 24
Cross Hill Glos 3C 71
Cross Houses Shrp 1A 44
Cross Lane Head Shrp 2C 45
Cross Lanes Wrex 3B 18
Crosslanes Shrp 3B 30
Cross o' th' Hands Derbs 3C 23
Crossway Mon 1B 70
Crossway Green Mon 3C 71
Crossway Green Worc 2C 57
Croughton Nptn 2B 68
Crowcroft Worc 3B 56
Crowdecote Derbs 1B 22
Crowden Derbs 1A 10
Crowfield Nptn 1C 69
Crow Hill Here 3A 64
Crowland Linc 3A 40
Crowle N Lin 2A 6
Crowle Worc 3D 57
Crowle Green Worc 3D 57
Croxall Staf 3B 34
Croxby Linc 1D 15
Croxden Staf 1A 34
Croxton N Lin 2D 7
Croxton Staf 1B 32
Croxtonbank Staf 1B 32
Croxton Green Ches E 2D 19
Croxton Kerrial Leics 2A 38
Cruckmeole Shrp 1D 43
Cruckton Shrp 3C 31
Crudgington Telf 3A 32
Crudwell Wilts 3C 73
Crug-y-byddar Powy 3A 42
Crumpsbrook Shrp 1A 56
Cubbington Warw 2D 59
Cubley Common Derbs 1B 34
Cublington Here 2B 62
Cuckney Notts 3B 12
Cuddington Heath Ches W 3C 19
Cudworth S Yor 3A 4
Culkerton Glos 3C 73
Culmington Shrp 3D 43
Culverthorpe Linc 3C 27
Culworth Nptn 1B 68
Cumberworth Linc 3D 17
Cumnor Oxon 2D 75
Curbar Derbs 3C 11
Curborough Staf 3B 34
Curbridge Oxon 2C 75
Curdworth Warw 2C 47
Cusop Here 1A 62
Cusworth S Yor 3C 5
Cutnall Green Worc 2C 57
Cutsdean Glos 2A 66
Cutthorpe Derbs 3D 11
Cuxwold Linc 3A 8
Cwm Powy 2B 42
Cwmcarvan Mon 2B 70
Cwmyoy Mon 3B 62
Cymau Flin 2A 18

D

Dadford Buck 2C 69
Dadlington Leics 2B 48
Dagdale Staf 1A 34
Daglingworth Glos 2C 73
Dagtail End Worc 2A 58
Daisy Bank W Mid 2B 46
Dalbury Derbs 1C 35
Dalby Wolds Leics 2C 37
Dalderby Linc 1A 28
Dale Abbey Derbs 1A 36
Dalebank Derbs 1D 23
Dalscote Nptn 3C 61
Dalton S Yor 1A 12
Dalton Magna S Yor 1A 12
Danebridge Ches E 1D 21
Danesford Shrp 2C 45
Danesmoor Derbs 1A 24
Danzey Green Warw 2B 58
Dapple Heath Staf 2A 34
Darfield S Yor 3B 4
Darlaston W Mid 2A 46
Darley Abbey Derb 1D 35
Darley Bridge Derbs 1C 23
Darley Dale Derbs 1C 23
Darlingscott Warw 1C 67
Darliston Shrp 1D 31
Darlton Notts 3D 13
Darnall S Yor 2D 11
Darnford Staf 1C 47
Darnhall Ches W 1A 20
Darrington W Yor 1B 4
Darton S Yor 2A 4
Daventry Nptn 2B 60
Dawley Telf 1B 44
Dawshill Worc 3C 57
Dawsmere Linc 1C 41
Dayhills Staf 1D 33
Dayhouse Bank Worc 1D 57
Daylesford Glos 3C 67
Daywall Shrp 1A 30
Dean Oxon 3D 67
Dean Park Shrp 2A 56
Deanshanger Nptn 1D 69
Deddington Oxon 2A 68
Deene Nptn 2C 51
Deenethorpe Nptn 2C 51
Deepcar S Yor 1C 11
Deepdale N Lin 2D 7
Deeping Gate Pet 1A 52
Deeping St James Linc 3D 39
Deeping St Nicholas Linc 3A 40
Deerhurst Glos 3C 65
Deerhurst Walton Glos 3C 65
Defford Worc 1D 65
Delamere Ches W 1D 19
Delly End Oxon 1C 75
Delves, The W Mid 2B 46
Dembleby Linc 1C 39
Denaby Main S Yor 1A 12
Denby Derbs 3D 23
Denby Common Derbs 3A 24
Denchworth Oxon 3C 75
Denstone Staf 3B 22
Denton Cambs 3A 52
Denton Linc 1A 38
Derby Derb 77 (1D 35)
Derrington Shrp 2B 44
Derrington Staf 2C 33
Derrythorpe N Lin 3B 6
Desborough Nptn 3B 50
Desford Leics 1B 48
Dethick Derbs 2D 23
Deuddwr Powy 3A 30
Devauden Mon 3B 70
Devitts Green Warw 2D 47
Dewsall Court Here 2C 63
Didbrook Glos 2A 66
Diddlebury Shrp 3A 44
Didley Here 2C 63
Digby Linc 2C 27
Dilhorne Staf 3D 21
Dilwyn Here 3C 55
Dinedor Here 2D 63
Dinedor Cross Here 2D 63
Dingestow Mon 1B 70
Dingley Nptn 3A 50
Dinnington S Yor 2B 12
Discoed Powy 2A 54
Diseworth Leics 2A 36
Ditton Priors Shrp 3B 44
Dixton Glos 2D 65
Dixton Mon 1C 71
Dobs Hill Flin 1B 18
Dobson's Bridge Shrp 1C 31
Docklow Here 3D 55
Doddenham Worc 3B 56
Doddington Cambs 2C 53
Doddington Linc 3B 14
Doddington Shrp 1A 56
Dodford Nptn 2C 61
Dodford Worc 1D 57
Dodleston Ches W 1B 18
Dods Leigh Staf 1A 34
Dodworth S Yor 3A 4
Doe Lea Derbs 1A 24
Dogdyke Linc 2A 28
Dogsthorpe Pet 1B 52
Doley Staf 2B 32
Dolfor Powy 3A 42
Dolley Green Powy 2A 54
Dolyhir Powy 3A 54
Domgay Powy 3A 30
Doncaster S Yor 3C 5
Doncaster Sheffield Airport S Yor 1C 13
Donington Linc 1A 40
Donington Shrp 1D 45
Donington Eaudike Linc 1A 40
Donington le Heath Leics 3A 36
Donington on Bain Linc 2A 16
Donington South Ing Linc 1A 40
Donisthorpe Leics 3D 35
Donna Nook Linc 1C 17
Donnington Glos 3B 66
Donnington Here 2B 64
Donnington Shrp 1A 44
Donnington Telf 3B 32
Dordon Warw 1D 47
Dore S Yor 2D 11
Dormington Here 1D 63
Dormston Worc 3D 57
Dorn Glos 2C 67
Dorridge W Mid 1B 58
Dorrington Linc 2C 27
Dorrington Shrp 1D 43
Dorsington Warw 1B 66
Dorstone Here 1B 62
Dosthill Staf 1D 47
Doughton Glos 3B 72
Dovaston Shrp 2B 30
Dove Holes Derbs 3A 10
Doverdale Worc 2C 57
Doveridge Derbs 1B 34
Dowdeswell Glos 1D 73
Dowles Worc 1B 56
Down, The Shrp 2B 44
Down Ampney Glos 3A 74
Down Hatherley Glos 3C 65
Downton on the Rock Here 1C 55
Dowsby Linc 2D 39
Dowsdale Linc 3A 40
Doxey Staf 2D 33
Dragonby N Lin 2C 7
Drakelow Worc 3D 45
Drakes Broughton Worc 1D 65
Drakes Cross Worc 1A 58
Draughton Nptn 1D 61
Drax N Yor 1D 5
Draycote Warw 1A 60
Draycott Derbs 1A 36
Draycott Glos 2B 66
Draycott Shrp 2D 45
Draycott Worc 1C 65
Draycott in the Clay Staf 2B 34
Draycott in the Moors Staf 3D 21
Drayton Leics 2B 50
Drayton Linc 1A 40
Drayton Nptn 2B 60
Drayton Oxon 3D 75
(nr Abingdon)
Drayton Oxon 1A 68
(nr Banbury)
Drayton Warw 3B 58
Drayton Worc 1D 57
Drayton Bassett Staf 1C 47
Drenewydd, Y Powy 2A 42
Driby Linc 3B 16
Driffield Glos 3D 73
Drointon Staf 2A 34
Droitwich Spa Worc 2C 57
Dronfield Derbs 3D 11
Dronfield Woodhouse Derbs 3D 11
Drugger's End Worc 2B 64
Druid's Heath W Mid 1B 46
Drury Flin 1A 18
Drybrook Glos 1D 71
Drybrook Here 1C 71
Dry Doddington Linc 3A 26
Dry Sandford Oxon 2D 75
Dryton Shrp 1A 44
Duckington Ches W 2C 19
Ducklington Oxon 2C 75
Duckmanton Derbs 3A 12
Dudbridge Glos 2B 72
Duddington Nptn 1C 51
Duddon Ches W 1D 19
Dudleston Shrp 1B 30
Dudleston Heath Shrp 1B 30
Dudley W Mid 3A 46
Dudston Shrp 2B 42
Duffield Derbs 3D 23
Dumbleton Glos 2A 66
Dunchurch Warw 1A 60
Duncote Nptn 3C 61
Dungworth S Yor 2C 11
Dunham-on-Trent Notts 3A 14
Dunhampton Worc 2C 57
Dunholme Linc 3C 15
Dunkirk Staf 2C 21
Dunley Worc 2B 56
Dunnington Warw 3A 58
Dunsby Linc 2D 39
Dunscroft S Yor 3D 5
Dunsley Staf 3D 45
Dunstal Staf 2A 34
Dunstall Staf 2B 34
Dunstall Hill W Mid 1A 46
Duns Tew Oxon 3A 68
Dunston Linc 1C 27
Dunston Staf 3D 33
Dunston Heath Staf 3D 33
Dunsville S Yor 3D 5
Duntisbourne Abbots Glos 2C 73
Duntisbourne Leer Glos 2C 73
Duntisbourne Rouse Glos 2C 73
Dunton Bassett Leics 2C 49
Dunwood Staf 2D 21
Durkar W Yor 2A 4
Durlow Common Here 2A 64
Dursley Glos 3A 72
Dursley Cross Glos 1D 71
Duston Nptn 2D 61
Dutlas Powy 1A 54
Duxford Oxon 3C 75
Dyke Linc 2D 39
Dymock Glos 2B 64

E

Eagle Linc 1A 26
Eagle Barnsdale Linc 1A 26
Eagle Moor Linc 1A 26
Eaglethorpe Nptn 2D 51
Eakring Notts 1C 25
Ealand N Lin 2A 6
Eardington Shrp 2C 45
Eardisland Here 3C 55
Eardisley Here 1B 62
Eardiston Shrp 2B 30
Eardiston Worc 2A 56
Earlesfield Linc 1B 38
Earl's Common Worc 3D 57
Earl's Croome Worc 1C 65
Earlsdon W Mid 1D 59
Earl Shilton Leics 2B 48
Earl Sterndale Derbs 1A 22
Earlswood Mon 3B 70
Earlswood Warw 1B 58
Easenhall Warw 1A 60
Easington E Yor 2C 9
Easington Oxon 2A 68
East Ardsley W Yor 1A 4
East Barkwith Linc 2D 15
East Bridgford Notts 3C 25
East Butterwick N Lin 3B 6
East Carlton Nptn 3B 50
East Claydon Buck 3D 69
Eastcombe Glos 2B 72
Eastcote Nptn 3C 61
Eastcote W Mid 1B 58
Eastcourt Wilts 3C 73
East Cowick E Yor 1D 5
East Dean Glos 3A 64
East Drayton Notts 3D 13
East Ella Hull 1D 7
East End E Yor 1B 8
East End Oxon 1C 75
East Farndon Nptn 3A 50
East Ferry Linc 1A 14
East Goscote Leics 3C 37
East Haddon Nptn 2C 61
East Halton N Lin 1A 8
Eastham Worc 2A 56
Easthampton Here 2C 55
East Hanney Oxon 3D 75
East Hardwick W Yor 2B 4
East Heckington Linc 3D 27
Easthope Shrp 2A 44
Easthorpe Leics 1A 38
Eastington Glos 1A 74
(nr Northleach)
Eastington Glos 2A 72
(nr Stonehouse)
East Keal Linc 1B 28
East Kirkby Linc 1B 28
East Langton Leics 2A 50
Eastleach Martin Glos 2B 74
Eastleach Turville Glos 2A 74
East Leake Notts 2B 36
East Lound N Lin 1D 13
East Markham Notts 3D 13
East Midlands Airport Leics 83 (2A 36)
Eastnor Here 2B 64
East Norton Leics 1A 50
Eastoft N Lin 2B 6
Easton Linc 2B 38
Easton on the Hill Nptn 1D 51
East Ravendale NE Lin 1A 16
Eastrea Cambs 2B 52
Eastrington E Yor 1A 6
East Stockwith Linc 1D 13
East Stoke Notts 3D 25
East Torrington Linc 2D 15
Eastville Linc 2C 29
East Wall Shrp 2A 44
Eastwell Leics 2D 37
Eastwood Notts 3A 24
Eastwood End Cambs 2D 53
Eathorpe Warw 2D 59
Eaton Ches E 1C 21
Eaton Ches W 1D 19
Eaton Leics 2D 37
Eaton Notts 3D 13
Eaton Oxon 2D 75
Eaton Shrp 3C 43
(nr Bishop's Castle)
Eaton Shrp 3A 44
(nr Church Stretton)
Eaton Bishop Here 2C 63
Eaton Constantine Shrp 1A 44
Eaton Hastings Oxon 3B 74
Eaton upon Tern Shrp 2A 32
Eau Brink Norf 3D 41
Eaves Green W Mid 3D 47
Ebley Glos 2B 72
Ebnal Ches W 3C 19
Ebrington Glos 1B 66
Ecclesall S Yor 2D 11
Ecclesfield S Yor 1D 11
Eccles Green Here 1B 62
Eccleshall Staf 2C 33
Eccleston Ches W 1C 19
Eckington Derbs 3A 12
Eckington Worc 1D 65
Edale Derbs 2B 10
Edenham Linc 2C 39
Edensor Derbs 3C 11
Edenthorpe S Yor 3D 5
Edgbaston W Mid 3B 46
Edgcott Buck 3C 69
Edge Glos 2B 72
Edge Shrp 1C 43
Edgebolton Shrp 2D 31
Edge End Glos 1C 71
Edge Green Ches W 2C 19
Edgeley Shrp 3D 19
Edgeworth Glos 2C 73
Edgiock Worc 2A 58
Edgmond Telf 3B 32
Edgmond Marsh Telf 2B 32
Edgton Shrp 3C 43
Edingale Staf 3C 35
Edingley Notts 2C 25
Edith Weston Rut 1C 51
Edlaston Derbs 3B 22
Edlington Linc 3A 16
Edmondthorpe Leics 3A 38
Ednaston Derbs 3C 23
Edstaston Shrp 1D 31
Edstone Warw 2B 58
Edwalton Notts 1B 36
Edwinstowe Notts 1C 25
Edwyn Ralph Here 3A 56
Efflinch Staf 3B 34
Egdon Worc 3D 57
Eggborough N Yor 1C 5
Egginton Derbs 2C 35
Egleton Rut 1B 50
Egmanton Notts 1D 25
Eldernell Cambs 2C 53
Eldersfield Worc 2C 65
Elford Staf 3B 34
Elkesley Notts 3C 13
Elkington Nptn 1C 61
Elkstone Glos 1C 73
Ellastone Staf 3B 22
Ellenhall Staf 2C 33
Ellerdine Telf 2A 32
Ellerdine Heath Telf 2A 32
Ellerker E Yor 1C 7
Ellerton Shrp 2B 32
Ellesmere Shrp 1C 31
Ellistown Leics 3A 36
Elloughton E Yor 1C 7
Ellwood Glos 2C 71
Elm Cambs 1D 53
Elmbridge Glos 1B 72
Elmbridge Worc 2D 57
Elmdon W Mid 3C 47
Elmdon Heath W Mid 3C 47
Elmesthorpe Leics 2B 48
Elmhurst Staf 3B 34
Elmley Castle Worc 1D 65
Elmley Lovett Worc 2C 57
Elmore Glos 1A 72
Elmore Back Glos 1A 72
Elmstone Hardwicke Glos 3D 65
Elmton Derbs 3B 12
Elsecar S Yor 1D 11
Elsham N Lin 2D 7
Elsthorpe Linc 2C 39
Elston Notts 3D 25
Elton Cambs 2D 51
Elton Derbs 1C 23
Elton Glos 1A 72
Elton Here 1C 55
Elton Notts 1D 37
Elvaston Derbs 1A 36
Elworth Ches E 1B 20
Emneth Norf 1D 53
Empingham Rut 1C 51
Enchmarsh Shrp 2A 44
Enderby Leics 2C 49
Endon Staf 2D 21
Endon Bank Staf 2D 21
Englesea-brook Ches E 2B 20
English Bicknor Glos 1C 71
English Frankton Shrp 2C 31
Ensdon Shrp 3C 31
Enson Staf 2D 33
Enstone Oxon 3D 67
Enville Staf 3D 45
Epney Glos 1A 72
Epperstone Notts 3C 25
Epwell Oxon 1D 67
Epworth N Lin 3A 6
Epworth Turbary N Lin 3A 6
Erbistock Wrex 3B 18
Erdington W Mid 2C 47
Eremine Linc 3B 14
Eryrys Den 2A 18
Eskham Linc 1B 16
Essendine Rut 3C 39
Essington Staf 1A 46
Etchinghill Staf 3A 34
Etloe Glos 2D 71
Ettiley Heath Ches E 1B 20
Ettington Warw 1C 67
Etton Pet 1A 52
Etwall Derbs 1C 35
Eudon Burnell Shrp 3C 45
Eudon George Shrp 3B 44
Evedon Linc 3C 27
Evendine Here 1B 64
Evenjobb Powy 2A 54
Evenley Nptn 2B 68
Evenlode Glos 3C 67
Everdon Nptn 3B 60
Everton Notts 1C 13
Evesbatch Here 1A 64
Evesham Worc 1A 66
Evington Leic 1D 49
Ewden Village S Yor 1C 11
Ewdness Shrp 2C 45
Ewen Glos 3D 73
Ewerby Linc 3D 27
Ewlo Flin 1A 18
Ewloe Flin 1A 18
Ewyas Harold Here 3B 62
Exfords Green Shrp 1D 43
Exhall Warw 3B 58
Exton Rut 3B 38
Eyam Derbs 3C 11
Eydon Nptn 3B 60
Eye Here 2C 55
Eye Pet 1B 52
Eye Green Pet 1B 52
Eynsham Oxon 2D 75
Eyton Here 2C 55
Eyton Shrp 3C 43
(nr Bishop's Castle)
Eyton Shrp 3B 30
(nr Shrewsbury)
Eyton Wrex 3B 18
Eyton on Severn Shrp 1A 44
Eyton upon the Weald Moors Telf 3A 32

F

Faddiley Ches E 2D 19
Fairburn N Yor 1B 4
Fairfield Derbs 3A 10
Fairfield Worc 1D 57
(nr Bromsgrove)
Fairfield Worc 1A 66
(nr Evesham)
Fairford Glos 2A 74
Fairoak Staf 1B 32
Falcon Here 2A 64
Faldingworth Linc 2C 15
Falfield S Glo 3D 71
Farcet Cambs 2B 52
Far Cotton Nptn 3D 61
Farewell Staf 3A 34
Far Forest Worc 1B 56
Farforth Linc 3B 16
Far Green Glos 2A 72
Far Hoarcross Staf 2B 34
Faringdon Oxon 3B 74
Farlesthorpe Linc 3C 17
Farley Shrp 1C 43
(nr Shrewsbury)
Farley Shrp 1B 44
(nr Telford)
Farley Staf 3A 22
Farleys End Glos 1A 72
Farlow Shrp 3B 44
Farmcote Glos 3A 66
Farmcote Shrp 2C 45
Farmington Glos 1A 74
Farmoor Oxon 2D 75
Farnah Green Derbs 3D 23
Farnborough Warw 1A 68
Farndon Ches W 2C 19
Farndon Notts 2D 25
Farnsfield Notts 2C 25

Far Oakridge – Hareby

Far Oakridge Glos 2C 73
Farthinghoe Nptn 2B 68
Farthingstone Nptn 3C 61
Farthorpe Linc 3A 16
Fauld Staf 2B 34
Fauls Shrp 1D 31
Fawfieldhead Staf 1A 22
Fawler Oxon 1C 75
Fawley Chapel Here 3D 63
Faxfleet E Yor 1B 6
Fazeley Staf 1C 47
Featherstone Staf 1A 46
Featherstone W Yor 1B 4
Feckenham Worc 2A 58
Felhampton Shrp 3D 43
Felindre Powy 3A 42
Felin Newydd Powy 2A 30
Felton Here 1D 63
Felton Butler Shrp 3B 30
Fen End Linc 2A 40
Fen End W Mid 1C 59
Fenhouses Linc 3A 28
Fenn Green Shrp 3C 45
Fenni, Y Mon 1A 70
Fenn's Bank Wrex 1D 31
Fenny Bentley Derbs 2B 22
Fenny Compton Warw 3A 60
Fenny Drayton Leics 2A 48
Fenton Linc 2A 26
(nr Caythorpe)
Fenton Linc 3A 14
(nr Saxilby)
Fenton Notts 2D 13
Fenton Stoke 3C 21
Fenwick S Yor 2C 5
Fernham Oxon 3B 74
Fernhill Heath Worc 3C 57
Fernilee Derbs 3A 10
Ferriby Sluice N Lin 1C 7
Ferrybridge W Yor 1B 4
Ferry Hill Cambs 3C 53
Fewcott Oxon 3B 68
Ffodun Powy 1B 42
Ffrith Flin 2A 18
Fiddington Glos 2D 65
Field Staf 1A 34
Field Assarts Oxon 1C 75
Field Head Leics 1B 48
Fifield Oxon 1B 74
Filkins Oxon 2B 74
Fillingham Linc 2B 14
Fillongley Warw 3D 47
Findern Derbs 1D 35
Finmere Oxon 2C 69
Finningley S Yor 1C 13
Finstall Worc 2D 57
Finstock Oxon 1C 75
Finwood Warw 2B 58
Firbeck S Yor 2B 12
Firsby Linc 1C 29
Fishlake S Yor 2D 5
Fishpool Glos 3A 64
Fishtoft Linc 3B 28
Fishtoft Drove Linc 3B 28
Fiskerton Linc 3C 15
Fiskerton Notts 2D 25
Fitton End Cambs 3C 41
Fitz Shrp 3C 31
Fitzwilliam W Yor 2B 4
Five Bridges Here 1A 64
Five Ways Warw 1C 59
Fladbury Worc 1D 65
Flagg Derbs 1B 22
Flash Staf 1A 22
Flawborough Notts 3D 25
Flaxholme Derbs 3D 23
Flaxley Glos 1D 71
Flaxley Green Staf 3A 34
Fleckney Leics 2D 49
Flecknoe Warw 2B 60
Fledborough Notts 3A 14
Fleet Linc 2B 40
Fleet Hargate Linc 2B 40
Flintham Notts 3D 25
Flintsham Here 3B 54
Flixborough N Lin 2B 6
Flood's Ferry Cambs 2C 53
Flore Nptn 2C 61
Flyford Flavell Worc 3D 57
Fockerby N Lin 2B 6
Fole Staf 1B 34
Foleshill W Mid 3A 48
Foley Park Worc 1C 57
Folkingham Linc 1C 39
Folksworth Cambs 3A 52
Foolow Derbs 3B 10
Footherley Staf 1C 47
Ford Derbs 2A 12
Ford Glos 3A 66
Ford Shrp 3C 31
Ford Staf 2A 22
Forden Powy 1B 42
Ford Heath Shrp 3C 31
Fordhouses W Mid 1A 46
Fordington Linc 3C 17
Fordwells Oxon 1C 75
Forebridge Staf 2D 33
Foremark Derbs 2D 35
Forest Green Glos 3B 72
Forest Town Notts 1B 24
Forge, The Here 3B 54
Forsbrook Staf 3D 21
Forthampton Glos 2C 65
Forthay Glos 3A 72
Forton Shrp 3C 31
Forton Staf 2B 32
Forton Heath Shrp 3C 31
Foscot Oxon 3C 67
Fosdyke Linc 1B 40
Fossebridge Glos 1D 73
Foston Derbs 1B 34
Foston Leics 2D 49
Foston Linc 3A 26
Fotherby Linc 1B 16
Fotheringhay Nptn 2D 51
Foul Anchor Cambs 3C 41
Four Ashes Staf 1A 46
(nr Cannock)
Four Ashes Staf 3D 45
(nr Kinver)
Four Crosses Powy 3A 30
Four Crosses Staf 1A 46
Four Gotes Cambs 3C 41
Fourlanes End Ches E 2C 21
Four Oaks Glos 3A 64
Four Oaks W Mid 3D 47
Fownhope Here 2D 63
Foxcote Glos 1D 73
Foxley Nptn 3C 61
Foxlydiate Worc 2A 58
Foxt Staf 3A 22
Foxton Leics 3D 49
Foxwist Green Ches W 1A 20
Foxwood Shrp 1A 56
Foy Here 3D 63
Fradley Staf 3B 34
Fradley South Staf 3B 34
Fradswell Staf 1D 33
Frampton Linc 1B 40
Frampton Mansell Glos 2C 73
Frampton on Severn Glos 2A 72
Frampton West End Linc 3A 28
Franche Worc 1C 57
Frankley Worc 3A 46
Frankton Warw 1A 60
Frankwell Shrp 3C 31
Freeby Leics 2A 38
Freehay Staf 3A 22
Freeland Oxon 1D 75
Freiston Linc 3B 28
Freiston Shore Linc 3B 28
Fretherne Glos 2A 72
Friday Bridge Cambs 1D 53
Friden Derbs 1B 22
Friesthorpe Linc 2C 15
Frieston Linc 3B 26
Friezeland Notts 2A 24
Frilford Oxon 3D 75
Fringford Oxon 3C 69
Frisby Leics 1A 50
Frisby on the Wreake Leics 3C 37
Friskney Linc 2C 29
Friskney Eaudyke Linc 2C 29
Fritchley Derbs 2D 23
Frith Bank Linc 3B 28
Frith Common Worc 2A 56
Frithville Linc 2B 28
Fritwell Oxon 3B 68
Frocester Glos 2A 72
Frochas Powy 1A 42
Frodesley Shrp 1A 44
Frodingham N Lin 2C 7
Froggatt Derbs 3C 11
Froghall Staf 3A 22
Frognall Linc 3D 39
Frolesworth Leics 2C 49
Fromes Hill Here 1A 64
Fron Powy 2A 42
(nr Newtown)
Fron Powy 1B 42
(nr Welshpool)
Froncysyllte Wrex 3A 18
Fron Isaf Wrex 3A 18
Fulbeck Linc 2B 26
Fulbrook Oxon 1B 74
Fulford Staf 1D 33
Fuller's Moor Ches W 2C 19
Fulletby Linc 3A 16
Fulnetby Linc 3C 15
Fulney Linc 2A 40
Fulstow Linc 1B 16
Fulwood Notts 2A 24
Fulwood S Yor 2C 11
Furness Vale Derbs 2A 10
Fyfield Glos 2B 74
Fyfield Oxon 3D 75

G

Gaddesby Leics 3C 37
Gagingwell Oxon 3A 68
Gailey Staf 3D 33
Gainsborough Linc 1A 14
Galley Common Warw 2A 48
Gallows Green Staf 3A 22
Gallows Green Worc 2D 57
Gamesley Derbs 1A 10
Gamston Notts 1C 37
(nr Nottingham)
Gamston Notts 3D 13
(nr Retford)
Ganarew Here 1C 71
Ganborough Glos 3B 66
Garden City Flin 1B 18
Garden Village S Yor 1C 11
Garford Oxon 3D 75
Garmelow Staf 2B 32
Garmston Shrp 1B 44
Garnsgate Linc 2C 41
Garshall Green Staf 1D 33
Garth Powy 1A 54
Garth Wrex 3A 18
Garthmyl Powy 2A 42
Garthorpe Leics 2A 38
Garthorpe N Lin 2B 6
Garth Owen Powy 2A 42
Garway Here 3C 63
Garway Common Here 3C 63
Garway Hill Here 3C 63
Garwick Linc 3D 27
Gate Burton Linc 2A 14
Gateforth N Yor 1C 5
Gatesheath Ches W 1C 19
Gaulby Leics 1D 49
Gaultree Norf 1D 53
Gautby Linc 3D 15
Gawber S Yor 3A 4
Gawcott Buck 2C 69
Gawsworth Ches E 1C 21
Gaydon Warw 3D 59
Gayton Nptn 3D 61
Gayton Staf 2D 33
Gayton le Marsh Linc 2C 17
Gayton le Wold Linc 2A 16
Geddington Nptn 3B 50
Gedling Notts 3C 25
Gedney Linc 2C 41
Gedney Broadgate Linc 2C 41
Gedney Drove End Linc 2C 41
Gedney Dyke Linc 2C 41
Gedney Hill Linc 3B 40
Geeston Rut 1C 51
Gelli Gandryll, Y Powy 1A 62
Gelston Linc 3B 26
Gentleshaw Staf 3A 34
Gerrard's Bromley Staf 1B 32
Geuffordd Powy 3A 30
Gibraltar Linc 2D 29
Gibsmere Notts 3D 25
Giggetty Staf 2D 45
Gilberdyke E Yor 1B 6
Gilbert's End Worc 1C 65
Gilbert's Green Warw 1B 58
Gildingwells S Yor 2B 12
Gillow Heath Staf 2C 21
Gilmorton Leics 3C 49
Giltbrook Notts 3A 24
Gipsey Bridge Linc 3A 28
Girton Notts 1A 26
Gladestry Powy 3A 54
Glanmule Powy 2A 42
Glapthorn Nptn 2D 51
Glapwell Derbs 1A 24
Glascoed Mon 2A 70
Glascote Staf 1D 47
Glasshouse Glos 3B 64
Glaston Rut 1B 50
Glatton Cambs 3A 52
Glazeley Shrp 3C 45
Gleadless S Yor 2D 11
Gleadsmoss Ches E 1C 21
Gledrid Shrp 1A 30
Glenfield Leics 1C 49
Glen Parva Leics 2C 49
Glentham Linc 1C 15
Glentworth Linc 2B 14
Glewstone Here 3D 63
Glinton Pet 1A 52
Glooston Leics 2A 50
Glossop Derbs 1A 10
Gloucester Glos 78 (1B 72)
Gloucestershire Airport Glos 3C 65
Glutton Bridge Derbs 1A 22
Glympton Oxon 3A 68
Glyn Ceiriog Wrex 1A 30
Gnosall Staf 2C 33
Gnosall Heath Staf 2C 33
Goadby Leics 2A 50
Goadby Marwood Leics 2D 37
Gobowen Shrp 1B 30
Godleybrook Staf 3D 21
Godstone Staf 1A 34
Goetre Mon 2A 70
Goldenhill Stoke 2C 21
Golden Valley Glos 3D 65
Golding Shrp 1A 44
Goldstone Shrp 2B 32
Goldthorpe S Yor 3B 4
Gonalston Notts 3C 25
Gonerby Hill Foot Linc 1B 38
Goodrich Here 1C 71
Goole E Yor 1A 6
Goom's Hill Worc 3A 58
Goosey Oxon 3C 75
Gorcott Hill Warw 2A 58
Gorefield Cambs 3C 41
Gornalwood W Mid 2A 46
Gorseybank Derbs 2C 23
Gorsley Glos 3A 64
Gorsley Common Here 3A 64
Gorstella Ches W 1B 18
Gorsty Common Here 2C 63
Gorsty Hill Staf 2B 34
Gosberton Linc 1A 40
Gosberton Cheal Linc 2A 40
Gosberton Clough Linc 2D 39
Goseley Dale Derbs 2D 35
Gospel End Staf 2D 45
Gossington Glos 2A 72
Gotham Notts 1B 36
Gotherington Glos 3D 65
Goulceby Linc 3A 16
Goverton Notts 3D 25
Gowdall E Yor 1D 5
Goxhill N Lin 1A 8
Goxhill Haven N Lin 1A 8
Graby Linc 2C 39
Grafton Here 2C 63
Grafton Oxon 2B 74
Grafton Shrp 3C 31
Grafton Worc 2D 65
(nr Evesham)
Grafton Worc 2D 55
(nr Leominster)
Grafton Flyford Worc 3D 57
Grafton Regis Nptn 1D 69
Grafton Underwood Nptn 3C 51
Graianrhyd Den 2A 18
Grainsby Linc 1A 16
Grainthorpe Linc 1B 16
Grainthorpe Fen Linc 1B 16
Graiselound N Lin 1D 13
Granborough Buck 3D 69
Granby Notts 1D 37
Grandborough Warw 2A 60
Grange Here 1C 55
Grangemill Derbs 2C 23
Grantham Linc 1B 38
Grasby Linc 3D 7
Grassmoor Derbs 1A 24
Grassthorpe Notts 1D 25
Gratton Staf 2D 21
Gratwich Staf 1A 34
Gravelhill Shrp 3C 31
Gravelly Hill W Mid 2C 47
Grayingham Linc 1B 14
Greasbrough S Yor 1A 12
Great Alne Warw 3B 58
Great Barr W Mid 2B 46
Great Barrington Glos 1B 74
Great Barrow Ches W 1C 19
Great Bolas Telf 2A 32
Great Bourton Oxon 1A 68
Great Bowden Leics 3A 50
Great Bridgeford Staf 2C 33
Great Brington Nptn 2C 61
Great Carlton Linc 2C 17
Great Casterton Rut 1C 51
Great Chatwell Staf 3B 32
Great Cliff W Yor 2A 4
Great Coates NE Lin 2B 8
Great Comberton Worc 1D 65
Great Coxwell Oxon 3B 74
Great Cubley Derbs 1B 34
Great Dalby Leics 3D 37
Great Doward Here 1C 71
Great Easton Leics 2B 50
Greatford Linc 3C 39
Great Gate Staf 3A 22
Great Gidding Cambs 3A 52
Great Glen Leics 2D 49
Great Gonerby Linc 1A 38
Great Hale Linc 3D 27
Great Haywood Staf 2D 33
Great Heath W Mid 3A 48
Great Heck N Yor 1C 5
Great Horwood Buck 2D 69
Great Houghton Nptn 3D 61
Great Houghton S Yor 3B 4
Great Hucklow Derbs 3B 10
Great Limber Linc 3A 8
Great Longstone Derbs 3C 11
Great Lyth Shrp 1D 43
Great Malvern Worc 1B 64
Great Ness Shrp 3B 30
Great Oak Mon 2A 70
Great Oakley Nptn 3B 50
Great Oxendon Nptn 3A 50
Great Ponton Linc 1B 38
Great Preston W Yor 1B 4
Great Raveley Cambs 3B 52
Great Rissington Glos 1A 74
Great Rollright Oxon 2D 67
Great Ryton Shrp 1D 43
Great Saredon Staf 1A 46
Great Steeping Linc 1C 29
Great Sturton Linc 3A 16
Great Sutton Shrp 3A 44
Great Tew Oxon 3D 67
Great Tows Linc 1A 16
Great Washbourne Glos 2D 65
Great Wilne Derbs 1A 36
Great Witcombe Glos 1C 73
Great Witley Worc 2B 56
Great Wolford Warw 2C 67
Greatworth Nptn 1B 68
Great Wyrley Staf 1A 46
Great Wytheford Shrp 3D 31
Grebby Linc 1C 29
Green End Warw 3D 47
Green Heath Staf 3D 33
Greenhill S Yor 2D 11
Greenhill Worc 1C 57
Greenlands Worc 2A 58
Green Lane Shrp 2A 32
Green Lane Worc 2A 58
Greens Norton Nptn 1C 69
Greet Glos 2A 66
Greete Shrp 1D 55
Greetham Linc 3B 16
Greetham Rut 3B 38
Grendon Warw 2D 47
Grendon Common Warw 2D 47
Grendon Green Here 3D 55
Grendon Underwood Buck 3C 69
Grenoside S Yor 1D 11
Gresford Wrex 2B 18
Gretton Glos 2A 66
Gretton Nptn 2C 51
Gretton Shrp 2A 44
Grey Green N Lin 3A 6
Greystones S Yor 2D 11
Griff Warw 3A 48
Griffydam Leics 3A 36
Grimethorpe S Yor 3B 4
Grimley Worc 2C 57
Grimoldby Linc 2B 16
Grimpo Shrp 2B 30
Grimsbury Oxon 1A 68
Grimsby NE Lin 3B 8
Grimscote Nptn 3C 61
Grimsthorpe Linc 2C 39
Grimston Leics 2C 37
Grindle Shrp 1C 45
Grindleford Derbs 3C 11
Grindley Staf 2A 34
Grindley Brook Shrp 3D 19
Grindlow Derbs 3B 10
Grindon Staf 2A 22
Gringley on the Hill Notts 1D 13
Grinshill Shrp 2D 31
Groby Leics 1C 49
Groes-lwyd Powy 3A 30
Grosmont Mon 3C 63
Grove Notts 3D 13
Grove Oxon 3C 75
Grove, The Worc 1C 65
Grub Street Staf 2B 32
Guarlford Worc 1C 65
Guilden Down Shrp 3C 43
Guilden Sutton Ches W 1C 19
Guilsborough Nptn 1C 61
Guilsfield Powy 3A 30
Guiting Power Glos 3A 66
Gumley Leics 2D 49
Gunby Linc 2B 38
Gunness N Lin 2B 6
Gunstone Staf 1D 45
Gunthorpe N Lin 1A 14
Gunthorpe Notts 3C 25
Gunthorpe Pet 1A 52
Guthram Gowt Linc 2D 39
Guyhirn Cambs 1D 53
Guyhirn Gull Cambs 1C 53
Guy's Head Linc 2C 41
Gwehelog Mon 2A 70
Gwernaffield Flin 1A 18
Gwernesney Mon 2B 70
Gwern-y-go Powy 2B 42
Gwernymynydd Flin 1A 18
Gwersyllt Wrex 2B 18
Gwynfryn Wrex 2A 18
Gyfelia Wrex 3B 18

H

Habberley Shrp 1D 43
Hablesthorpe Notts 2D 13
Habrough NE Lin 2A 8
Haceby Linc 1C 39
Hackenthorpe S Yor 2A
Hackman's Gate Worc 1C
Hackthorn Linc 2B
Haconby Linc 2D
Haddington Linc 1B
Haddon Cambs 2A
Hademore Staf 1C
Hadfield Derbs 1A
Hadley Telf 3A
Hadley Worc 2C
Hadley End Staf 2B
Hadnall Shrp 2D
Hady Derbs 3D
Hadzor Worc 2D
Hagley Here 1D
Hagley Worc 3A
Hagnaby Linc 1B
Hagworthingham Linc 1B
Hailes Glos 2A
Hailey Oxon 1C
Hainton Linc 2D
Halam Notts 2C
Hales Staf 1B
Halesgate Linc 2B
Hales Green Derbs 3B
Halesowen W Mid 3A
Halford Shrp 3D
Halford Warw 1C
Halfpenny Green Staf 2D
Halfway S Yor 2A
Halfway House Shrp 3B
Hallam Fields Derbs 3A
Hallands, The N Lin 1D
Hallaton Leics 2A
Hall Green Ches E 2C
Hall Green W Mid 3C
Hall Green W Yor 2A
Hall Green Wrex 3C
Hallington Linc 2B
Halloughton Notts 2C
Hallow Worc 3C
Hallow Heath Worc 3C
Hallowsgate Ches W 1D
Hallwood Green Glos 2A
Halmer End Staf 3C
Halmond's Frome Here 1A
Halmore Glos 2D
Halse Nptn 1B
Halsham E Yor 1B
Halstead Leics 1A
Haltham Linc 1A
Haltoft End Linc 3B
Halton Wrex 1B
Halton Fenside Linc 1C
Halton Holegate Linc 1C
Ham Glos 3D
Hameringham Linc 1B
Ham Green Here 1B
Ham Green Worc 2A
Hamilton Leic 1D
Hammerwich Staf 1B
Hampen Glos 1D
Hamperley Shrp 3D
Hampnett Glos 1D
Hampole S Yor 2C
Hampton Shrp 3C
Hampton Swin 3A
Hampton Worc 1A
Hampton Bishop Here 2D
Hampton Fields Glos 3B
Hampton Hargate Pet 2A
Hampton Heath Ches W 3D
Hampton in Arden W Mid 3D
Hampton Loade Shrp 3C
Hampton Lovett Worc 2C
Hampton Lucy Warw 3C
Hampton Magna Warw 2C
Hampton on the Hill Warw 2C
Hamstall Ridware Staf 3B
Hamstead W Mid 2B
Hanbury Staf 2B
Hanbury Worc 2D
Hanbury Woodend Staf 2B
Hanby Linc 1C
Hanchurch Staf 3C
Handbridge Ches W 1C
Handley Ches W 2C
Handley Derbs 1D
Handsacre Staf 3A
Handsworth S Yor 2A
Handsworth W Mid 2B
Hanford Stoke 3C
Hanging Houghton Nptn 1D
Hankelow Ches E 3A
Hankerton Wilts 3C
Hanley Stoke 3C
Hanley Castle Worc 1C
Hanley Child Worc 2A
Hanley Swan Worc 1C
Hanley William Worc 2A
Hanmer Wrex 1C
Hannah Linc 3D
Hannington Swin 3A
Hannington Wick Swin 3A
Hanthorpe Linc 2C
Hanwell Oxon 1A
Hanwood Shrp 1D
Harborne W Mid 3B
Harborough Magna Warw 1A
Harbours Hill Worc 2D
Harbury Warw 2D
Harby Leics 1D
Harby Notts 3A
Hardingstone Nptn 3D
Hardings Wood Staf 2C
Hardstoft Derbs 1A
Hardwick Oxon 3B
(nr Bicest
Hardwick Oxon 2C
(nr Witn
Hardwick S Yor 2A
Hardwick Shrp 2C
Hardwick W Mid 2B
Hardwicke Glos 3D
(nr Cheltenha
Hardwicke Glos 1A
(nr Glouces
Hardwicke Here 1A
Hardwick Village Notts 3C
Hareby Linc 1B

King's Stanley – Lyonshall

King's Stanley *Glos* 2B 72
King's Sutton *Nptn* 2A 68
Kingstanding *W Mid* 2B 46
King Sterndale *Derbs* 3A 10
King's Thorn *Here* 2D 63
Kingsthorpe *Nptn* 2D 61
Kingston Bagpuize *Oxon* 3D 75
Kingstone *Here* 2C 63
Kingstone *Staf* 2A 34
Kingston on Soar *Notts* 2B 36
Kingston upon Hull *Hull* 1A 8
Kingswinford *W Mid* 3D 45
Kingswood *Glos* 3A 72
Kingswood *Here* 3A 54
Kingswood *Powy* 1B 42
Kingswood *Warw* 1B 58
Kingswood Common *Staf* 1D 45
Kingthorpe *Linc* 3D 15
Kington *Here* 3A 54
Kington *S Glo* 3D 71
Kington *Worc* 3D 57
Kinlet *Shrp* 3C 45
Kinnerley *Shrp* 2B 30
Kinnersley *Here* 1B 62
Kinnersley *Worc* 1C 65
Kinnerton *Powy* 2A 54
Kinnerton *Shrp* 2C 43
Kinoulton *Notts* 1C 37
Kinsey Heath *Ches E* 3A 20
Kinsham *Here* 2B 54
Kinsham *Worc* 2D 65
Kinsley *W Yor* 2B 4
Kinton *Here* 1C 55
Kinton *Shrp* 3B 30
Kinver *Staf* 3D 45
Kinwarton *Warw* 3B 58
Kirby Bellars *Leics* 3D 37
Kirby Fields *Leics* 1C 49
Kirby Muxloe *Leics* 1C 49
Kirk Bramwith *S Yor* 2D 5
Kirkby *Linc* 1C 15
Kirkby Fenside *Linc* 1B 28
Kirkby Green *Linc* 2C 27
Kirkby-in-Ashfield *Notts* 2B 24
Kirkby la Thorpe *Linc* 3D 27
Kirkby Mallory *Leics* 1B 48
Kirkby on Bain *Linc* 1A 28
Kirkby Underwood *Linc* 2C 39
Kirk Ella *E Yor* 1D 7
Kirk Hallam *Derbs* 3A 24
Kirk Ireton *Derbs* 2C 23
Kirk Langley *Derbs* 1C 35
Kirklington *Notts* 2C 25
Kirk Sandall *S Yor* 3D 5
Kirk Smeaton *N Yor* 2C 5
Kirkthorpe *W Yor* 1A 4
Kirmington *N Lin* 2A 8
Kirmond le Mire *Linc* 1D 15
Kirton *Linc* 1B 40
Kirton *Notts* 1C 25
Kirton End *Linc* 3A 28
Kirton Holme *Linc* 3A 28
Kirton in Lindsey *N Lin* 1B 14
Kislingbury *Nptn* 3C 61
Kites Hardwick *Warw* 2A 60
Kivernoll *Here* 2C 63
Kiveton Park *S Yor* 2A 12
Knaith *Linc* 2A 14
Knaith Park *Linc* 2A 14
Knapton Green *Here* 3C 55
Knedlington *E Yor* 1A 6
Kneesall *Notts* 1D 25
Kneeton *Notts* 3D 25
Knenhall *Staf* 1D 33
Knightcote *Warw* 3A 60
Knightley *Staf* 2C 33
Knightley Dale *Staf* 2C 33
Knightlow Hill *Warw* 1A 60
Knighton *Leic* 1C 49
Knighton *Powy* 1A 54
Knighton *Staf* 2B 32
(nr Eccleshall)
Knighton *Staf* 3B 20
(nr Woore)
Knighton *Worc* 3A 58
Knighton Common *Worc* 1A 56
Knight's End *Cambs* 2D 53
Knightwick *Worc* 3B 56
Knill *Here* 2A 54
Knipton *Leics* 1A 38
Kniveton *Derbs* 2B 23
Knockin *Shrp* 2B 30
Knolton *Wrex* 1B 30
Knossington *Leics* 1B 50
Knottingley *W Yor* 1B 4
Knowbury *Shrp* 1D 55
Knowle *Shrp* 1D 55
Knowle *W Mid* 1B 58
Knowlesands *Shrp* 2C 45
Knucklas *Powy* 1A 54
Knypersley *Staf* 2C 21
Kymin *Mon* 1C 71
Kynaston *Here* 2A 64
Kynaston *Shrp* 2B 30
Kynnersley *Telf* 3A 32
Kyre Green *Worc* 2A 56
Kyre Park *Worc* 2A 56
Kyrewood *Worc* 2A 56

L

Laceby *NE Lin* 3B 8
Lache *Ches W* 1B 18
Ladbroke *Warw* 3A 60
Lade Bank *Linc* 2B 28
Ladywood *W Mid* 3B 46
Ladywood *Worc* 2C 57
Lambley *Notts* 3C 25
Lamport *Nptn* 1D 61
Landywood *Staf* 1A 46
Lane Ends *Derbs* 1C 35
Laneham *Notts* 3A 14
Laney Green *Staf* 1A 46
Langar *Notts* 1D 37
Langford *Notts* 2A 26
Langford *Oxon* 2B 74
Langham *Rut* 3A 38
Langley *Derbs* 3A 24
Langley *Glos* 3A 66
Langley *Warw* 2B 58
Langley Common *Derbs* 1C 35
Langley Green *Derbs* 1C 35
Langley Green *Warw* 2B 58
Langold *Notts* 2B 12
Langrick *Linc* 3A 28
Langtoft *Linc* 3D 39
Langton *Linc* 1A 28
(nr Horncastle)
Langton *Linc* 3B 16
(nr Spilsby)
Langton by Wragby *Linc* 3D 15
Langwith *Derbs* 3B 12
Langworth *Linc* 3C 15
Lansdown *Glos* 3D 65
Lapley *Staf* 3C 33
Lapworth *Warw* 1B 58
Larden Green *Ches E* 2D 19
Larport *Here* 2D 63
Latton *Wilts* 3D 73
Laughterton *Linc* 3A 14
Laughton *Leics* 3D 49
Laughton *Linc* 1A 14
(nr Gainsborough)
Laughton *Linc* 1C 39
(nr Grantham)
Laughton Common *S Yor* 2B 12
Laughton en le Morthen *S Yor* 2B 12
Launton *Oxon* 3C 69
Laverton *Glos* 2A 66
Lavister *Wrex* 2B 18
Lawley *Telf* 1B 44
Lawnhead *Staf* 2C 33
Lawton *Here* 3C 55
Laxton *E Yor* 1A 6
Laxton *Notts* 1D 25
Laxton *Nptn* 2C 51
Laysters Pole *Here* 2D 55
Lea *Derbs* 2D 23
Lea *Here* 3A 64
Lea *Linc* 2A 14
Lea *Shrp* 3C 43
(nr Bishop's Castle)
Lea *Shrp* 1D 43
(nr Shrewsbury)
Leabrooks *Derbs* 2A 24
Leadenham *Linc* 2B 26
Lea End *Worc* 1A 58
Leafield *Oxon* 1C 75
Lea Hall *W Mid* 3C 47
Lea Heath *Staf* 2A 34
Leake Common Side *Linc* 2B 28
Leake Fold Hill *Linc* 2C 29
Leake Hurn's End *Linc* 3C 29
Leam *Derbs* 3C 11
Lea Marston *Warw* 2D 47
Leamington Hastings *Warw* 2A 60
Leamington Spa, Royal *Warw* 2D 59
Leamonsley *Staf* 1C 47
Leasingham *Linc* 3C 27
Leaton *Shrp* 3C 31
Leaton *Telf* 3A 32
Lechlade on Thames *Glos* 3B 74
Leckhampstead *Buck* 2D 69
Leckhampton *Glos* 1C 73
Ledbury *Here* 2B 64
Ledgemoor *Here* 3C 55
Ledicot *Here* 2C 55
Ledsham *W Yor* 1B 4
Ledston *W Yor* 1B 4
Ledwell *Oxon* 3A 68
Lee *Shrp* 1C 31
Leebotwood *Shrp* 2D 43
Lee Brockhurst *Shrp* 2D 31
Leegomery *Telf* 3A 32
Lee Head *Derbs* 1A 10
Leek *Staf* 2D 21
Leekbrook *Staf* 2D 21
Leek Wootton *Warw* 2C 59
Lee Moor *W Yor* 1A 4
Lees *Derbs* 1C 35
Leeswood *Flin* 1A 18
Legbourne *Linc* 2B 16
Legsby *Linc* 2D 15
Leicester *Leic* 78 (1C 49)
Leicester Forest East *Leics* 1C 49
Leigh *Shrp* 1C 43
Leigh *Wilts* 3D 73
Leigh *Worc* 3B 56
Leigh, The *Glos* 3C 65
Leigh Sinton *Worc* 3B 56
Leighterton *Glos* 3B 72
Leighton *Powy* 1B 42
Leighton *Shrp* 1B 44
Leinthall Earls *Here* 2C 55
Leinthall Starkes *Here* 2C 55
Leintwardine *Here* 1C 55
Leire *Leics* 2C 49
Lem Hill *Shrp* 1B 56
Lenchwick *Worc* 1A 66
Lenton *Linc* 1C 39
Leominster *Here* 3C 55
Leonard Stanley *Glos* 2B 72
Letton *Here* 1B 62
(nr Kington)
Letton *Here* 1B 54
(nr Leintwardine)
Letwell *S Yor* 2B 12
Levedale *Staf* 3C 33
Leverington *Cambs* 3C 41
Leverton *Linc* 3B 28
Leverton Lucasgate *Linc* 3C 29
Leverton Outgate *Linc* 3C 29
Lew *Oxon* 2C 75
Leycett *Staf* 3B 20
Leyfields *Staf* 1D 47
Libbery *Worc* 3D 57
Lichfield *Staf* 1C 47
Lickey *Worc* 1D 57
Lickey End *Worc* 1D 57
Lidgett *Notts* 1C 25
Lidstone *Oxon* 3D 67
Lifford *W Mid* 3B 46
Lighthorne *Warw* 3D 59
Light Oaks *Stoke* 2D 21
Lightwood *Staf* 3A 22
Lightwood *Stoke* 3D 21
Lightwood Green *Ches E* 3A 20
Lightwood Green *Wrex* 3B 18
Lilbourne *Nptn* 1B 60
Lilleshall *Telf* 3B 32
Lillingstone Dayrell *Buck* 2D 69
Lillingstone Lovell *Buck* 1D 69
Lilyhurst *Shrp* 3B 32
Lime Street *Worc* 2C 65
Linby *Notts* 3C 63
Lincoln *Linc* 79 (3B 14)
Lincomb *Worc* 2C 57
Linden *Glos* 1B 72
Lindridge *Worc* 2A 56
Lingen *Here* 2B 54
Linkend *Worc* 2C 65
Linley *Shrp* 2C 43
(nr Bishop's Castle)
Linley *Shrp* 2B 44
(nr Bridgnorth)
Linley Green *Here* 3A 56
Linton *Derbs* 3C 35
Linton *Here* 3A 64
Linton Hill *Here* 3A 64
Linwood *Linc* 2D 15
Lipley *Shrp* 1B 32
Lissington *Linc* 2D 15
Litchborough *Nptn* 3C 61
Little Airmyn *N Yor* 1A 6
Little Alne *Warw* 2B 58
Little Aston *Staf* 1B 46
Little Barrington *Glos* 1B 74
Little Barrow *Ches W* 1C 19
Little Birch *Here* 2D 63
Little Bolas *Shrp* 2A 32
Littleborough *Notts* 2A 14
Little Bourton *Oxon* 1A 68
Little Bowden *Leics* 3A 50
Little Brampton *Shrp* 3C 43
Little Bridgeford *Staf* 2C 33
Little Brington *Nptn* 2C 61
Little Budworth *Ches W* 1D 19
Little Bytham *Linc* 3C 39
Little Carlton *Linc* 2B 16
Little Carlton *Notts* 2D 25
Little Casterton *Rut* 1D 51
Little Cawthorpe *Linc* 2B 16
Little Clanfield *Oxon* 2B 74
Little Coates *NE Lin* 3B 8
Little Comberton *Worc* 1D 65
Little Compton *Warw* 2C 67
Little Cowarne *Here* 3A 56
Little Coxwell *Oxon* 3B 74
Little Cubley *Derbs* 1B 34
Little Dalby *Leics* 3D 37
Little Dawley *Telf* 1B 44
Littledean *Glos* 1D 71
Little Dewchurch *Here* 2D 63
Little Drayton *Shrp* 1A 32
Little Eaton *Derbs* 3D 23
Little Everdon *Nptn* 3B 60
Little Faringdon *Oxon* 2B 74
Little Garway *Here* 3C 63
Little Gidding *Cambs* 3A 52
Little Green *Wrex* 3C 19
Little Grimsby *Linc* 1B 16
Little Hale *Linc* 3D 27
Little Haresfield *Glos* 2B 72
Little Hay *Staf* 1C 47
Little Hayfield *Derbs* 2A 10
Little Haywood *Staf* 2A 34
Little Heath *W Mid* 3A 48
Little Heck *N Yor* 1C 5
Little Herbert's *Glos* 1C 73
Little Hereford *Here* 2D 55
Little Horwood *Buck* 2D 69
Little Houghton *S Yor* 3B 4
Little Hucklow *Derbs* 3B 10
Little Kineton *Warw* 3D 59
Little Lawford *Warw* 1A 60
Little London *Linc* 2C 41
(nr Long Sutton)
Little London *Linc* 2A 40
(nr Spalding)
Little Longstone *Derbs* 3B 10
Little Malvern *Worc* 1B 64
Little Marcle *Here* 2A 64
Little Mill *Mon* 2A 70
Littlemoor *Derbs* 1D 23
Little Mountain *Flin* 1A 18
Little Ness *Shrp* 3C 31
Little Oakley *Nptn* 3B 50
Little Onn *Staf* 3C 33
Little Orton *Leics* 1A 48
Littleover *Derb* 1D 35
Little Packington *Warw* 3D 47
Little Ponton *Linc* 1B 38
Little Preston *Nptn* 3B 60
Little Rissington *Glos* 1A 74
Little Rollright *Oxon* 2C 67
Little Ryton *Shrp* 1D 43
Little Saredon *Staf* 1A 46
Little Smeaton *N Yor* 2C 5
Little Soudley *Shrp* 2B 32
Little Steeping *Linc* 1C 29
Little Stoke *Staf* 1D 33
Little Stretton *Leics* 1D 49
Little Stretton *Shrp* 2D 43
Little Sugnall *Staf* 1C 33
Little Sutton *Linc* 2C 41
Little Tew *Oxon* 3D 67
Littlethorpe *Leics* 2C 49
Littleton *Ches W* 1C 19
Little Twycross *Leics* 1A 48
Little Wenlock *Telf* 1B 44
Little Wisbeach *Linc* 1D 39
Little Witcombe *Glos* 1C 73
Little Witley *Worc* 2B 56
Little Wolford *Warw* 2C 67
Littleworth *Glos* 2B 66
Littleworth *Oxon* 3C 75
Littleworth *Staf* 3A 34
(nr Cannock)
Littleworth *Staf* 2B 32
(nr Eccleshall)
Littleworth *Staf* 2D 33
(nr Stafford)
Littleworth *Worc* 2D 57
(nr Redditch)
Littleworth *Worc* 3C 57
(nr Worcester)
Little Wyrley *Staf* 1B 46
Litton *Derbs* 3B 10
Llanandras *Powy* 2B 54
Llanarth *Mon* 1A 70
Llanbadoc *Mon* 2A 70
Llanbeder *Newp* 3A 70
Llanbedr *Powy* 3A 62
Llancayo *Mon* 2A 70
Llancloudy *Here* 3C 63
Llancoch *Powy* 1A 54
Llanddewi Rhydderch *Mon* 1A 70
Llandegveth *Mon* 3A 70
Llandenny *Mon* 2B 70
Llandevaud *Newp* 3B 70
Llandinabo *Here* 3D 63
Llandogo *Mon* 2C 71
Llandrinio *Powy* 3A 30
Llandysilio *Powy* 3A 30
Llandyssil *Powy* 2A 42
Llanellen *Mon* 1A 70
Llanerch *Powy* 2C 43
Llanfaenor *Mon* 1B 70
Llanfair *Here* 1A 62
Llanfair Caereinion *Powy* 1A 42
Llanfair Waterdine *Shrp* 1A 54
Llanfihangel Ystum Llewern *Mon* 1B 70
Llanfrechfa *Torf* 3A 70
Llanfynydd *Flin* 2A 18
Llangarron *Here* 3D 63
Llangattock Lingoed *Mon* 3B 62
Llangattock-Vibon-Avel *Mon* 1B 70
Llangollen *Den* 3A 18
Llangovan *Mon* 2B 70
Llangrove *Here* 1C 71
Llangua *Mon* 3B 62
Llangunllo *Powy* 1A 54
Llan-gwm *Mon* 2B 70
Llan-gwm-isaf *Mon* 2B 70
Llangybi *Mon* 3A 70
Llanhennock *Mon* 3A 70
Llanigon *Powy* 1A 62
Llanishen *Mon* 2B 70
Llanllowell *Mon* 3A 70
Llanllwchaiarn *Powy* 2A 42
Llanmerwig *Powy* 2A 42
Llanover *Mon* 2A 70
Llanrothal *Here* 1B 70
Llansantffraid-ym-Mechain *Powy* 2A 30
Llansilin *Powy* 2A 30
Llansoy *Mon* 2B 70
Llantarnam *Torf* 3A 70
Llanthony *Mon* 3A 62
Llantilio Crossenny *Mon* 1A 70
Llantilio Pertholey *Mon* 1A 70
Llantrisant *Mon* 3A 70
Llanvaches *Newp* 3B 70
Llanvair Discoed *Mon* 3B 70
Llanvapley *Mon* 1A 70
Llanvetherine *Mon* 1A 70
Llanveynoe *Here* 2B 62
Llanvihangel Crucorney *Mon* 3B 62
Llanvihangel Gobion *Mon* 2A 70
Llanwarne *Here* 3D 63
Llanyblodwel *Shrp* 2A 30
Llanymynech *Powy* 2A 30
Llan-y-pwll *Wrex* 2B 18
Llanyrafon *Torf* 3A 70
Llawnt *Shrp* 1A 30
Llay *Wrex* 2B 18
Llechrydau *Wrex* 1A 30
Llong *Flin* 1A 18
Lloyney *Powy* 1A 54
Llwynderw *Powy* 1B 42
Llwynmawr *Wrex* 1A 30
Llynclys *Shrp* 2A 30
Lockington *Leics* 2A 36
Lockleywood *Shrp* 2A 32
Loddington *Leics* 1A 50
Lofthouse *W Yor* 1A 4
Lofthouse Gate *W Yor* 1A 4
Logaston *Here* 3B 54
Loggerheads *Staf* 1B 32
Londonthorpe *Linc* 1B 38
Long Bank *Worc* 1B 56
Long Bennington *Linc* 3A 26
Longborough *Glos* 3B 66
Longbridge *W Mid* 1A 58
Longbridge *Warw* 2C 59
Long Buckby *Nptn* 2C 61
Long Buckby Wharf *Nptn* 2C 61
Long Clawson *Leics* 2D 37
Longcliffe *Derbs* 2C 23
Long Compton *Staf* 2C 33
Long Compton *Warw* 2C 67
Longcot *Oxon* 3B 74
Longden *Shrp* 1D 43
Longden Common *Shrp* 1D 43
Longdon *Staf* 3A 34
Longdon *Worc* 2C 65
Longdon Green *Staf* 3A 34
Longdon on Tern *Telf* 3A 32
Long Drax *N Yor* 1D 5
Long Duckmanton *Derbs* 3A 12
Long Eaton *Derbs* 1A 36
Longford *Derbs* 1C 35
Longford *Glos* 3C 65
Longford *Shrp* 1A 32
Longford *Telf* 3B 32
Longford *W Mid* 3A 48
Long Green *Worc* 2C 65
Long Hanborough *Oxon* 1D 75
Longhope *Glos* 1D 71
Long Itchington *Warw* 2A 60
Long Lane *Telf* 3A 32
Longlane *Derbs* 1C 35
Long Lawford *Warw* 1A 60
Longley Green *Worc* 3B 56
Long Marston *Warw* 1B 66
Long Meadowend *Shrp* 3D 43
Long Newnton *Glos* 3C 73
Longney *Glos* 1A 72
Longnor *Shrp* 1D 43
Longnor *Staf* 1A 22
(nr Leek)
Longnor *Staf* 3C 33
(nr Stafford)
Longridge *Staf* 3D 33
Longsdon *Staf* 2D 21
Longshaw *Staf* 3A 22
Longslow *Shrp* 1A 32
Long Street *Mil* 1D 69
Long Sutton *Linc* 2C 41
Longthorpe *Pet* 2A 52
Longton *Stoke* 3D 21
Longtown *Here* 3B
Longville in the Dale *Shrp* 2A
Long Whatton *Leics* 2A
Longworth *Oxon* 3C
Loosegate *Linc* 2B
Loppington *Shrp* 2C
Loscoe *Derbs* 3A
Loughborough *Leics* 3B
Loughton *Shrp* 3B
Lound *Linc* 3C
Lound *Notts* 2C
Lount *Leics* 3D
Louth *Linc* 2B
Loversall *S Yor* 1B
Low Ackworth *W Yor* 2B
Lowbands *Glos* 2B
Low Barlings *Linc* 3C
Low Bradfield *S Yor* 1C
Low Burnham *N Lin* 3A
Lowdham *Notts* 3C
Lowe *Shrp* 1D
Lower Benefield *Nptn* 3C
Lower Bentley *Worc* 2D
Lower Beobridge *Shrp* 2C
Lower Boddington *Nptn* 3A
Lower Brailes *Warw* 2D
Lower Broadheath *Worc* 3C
Lower Bullingham *Here* 2D
Lower Cam *Glos* 2A
Lower Catesby *Nptn* 3B
Lower Clopton *Warw* 3B
Lower Crossings *Derbs* 2A
Lower Down *Shrp* 3C
Lower Egleton *Here* 1A
Lower Ellastone *Staf* 3B
Lower Faintree *Shrp* 3B
Lower Frankton *Shrp* 1B
Lower Hardwick *Here* 3C
Lower Hartshay *Derbs* 2D
Lower Hayton *Shrp* 3A
Lower Hergest *Here* 3A
Lower Heyford *Oxon* 3A
Lower Hordley *Shrp* 2B
Lower Kinnerton *Ches W* 1B
Lower Ledwyche *Shrp* 1D
Lower Leigh *Staf* 1A
Lower Lemington *Glos* 2C
Lower Ley *Glos* 1A
Lower Lode *Glos* 2C
Lower Loxley *Staf* 1A
Lower Lydbrook *Glos* 1C
Lower Lye *Here* 2C
Lower Maes-coed *Here* 2B
Lower Meend *Glos* 2C
Lower Midway *Derbs* 2D
Lower Moor *Worc* 1D
Lower Morton *S Glo* 3D
Lower Mountain *Flin* 2B
Lower Netchwood *Shrp* 2B
Lower Oddington *Glos* 3C
Lower Penn *Staf* 2D
Lower Pilsley *Derbs* 1A
Lower Quinton *Warw* 1B
Lower Shuckburgh *Warw* 2A
Lower Slaughter *Glos* 3B
Lower Soudley *Glos* 1D
Lower Stonnall *Staf* 1B
Lower Strensham *Worc* 1D
Lower Swell *Glos* 3B
Lower Tean *Staf* 1A
Lower Thurvaston *Derbs* 1C
Lower Town *Here* 1A
Lower Tysoe *Warw* 1D
Lower Welson *Here* 3A
Lower Withington *Ches E* 1C
Lower Wych *Ches W* 3C
Lower Wyche *Worc* 1B
Lowesby *Leics* 1A
Low Fulney *Linc* 2A
Low Habberley *Worc* 1C
Low Hameringham *Linc* 1B
Lowick *Nptn* 3C
Low Leighton *Derbs* 2A
Low Marnham *Notts* 1A
Lowsonford *Warw* 2B
Low Toynton *Linc* 3A
Loxley *S Yor* 2D
Loxley *Warw* 3C
Loxley Green *Staf* 1A
Lubenham *Leics* 3A
Lucton *Here* 2C
Ludborough *Linc* 1A
Luddington *N Lin* 2B
Luddington *Warw* 3B
Luddington in the Brook *Nptn* 3A
Ludford *Linc* 2D
Ludford *Shrp* 1D
Ludlow *Shrp* 1D
Ludstone *Shrp* 2D
Lugg Green *Here* 2C
Lugwardine *Here* 1D
Lulham *Here* 1C
Lullington *Derbs* 3C
Lulsley *Worc* 3B
Lupset *W Yor* 2A
Lusby *Linc* 1B
Luston *Here* 2C
Lutley *Staf* 3D
Lutterworth *Leics* 3C
Lutton *Linc* 2C
Lutton *Nptn* 3A
Lutton Gowts *Linc* 2C
Luxley *Glos* 3A
Lydbury North *Shrp* 3C
Lyddington *Rut* 2B
Lydham *Shrp* 2C
Lydiate Ash *Worc* 1D
Lydney *Glos* 2D
Lye *W Mid* 3A
Lye, The *Shrp* 2B
Lye Head *Worc* 1B
Lyford *Oxon* 3C
Lyndon *Rut* 1C
Lyneal *Shrp* 1C
Lyne Down *Here* 2A
Lyneham *Oxon* 3C
Lynn *Staf* 1B
Lynn *Telf* 3B
Lyonshall *Here* 3B

Mablethorpe – North Aston

M

Mablethorpe *Linc* 2D 17
Mackworth *Derb* 1D 35
Madeley *Staf* 3B 20
Madeley *Telf* 1B 44
Madeley Heath *Staf* 3B 20
Madeley Heath *Worc* 1D 57
Madley *Here* 2C 63
Madresfield *Worc* 1C 65
Maer *Staf* 1B 32
Maesbrook *Shrp* 2B 30
Maesbury *Shrp* 2B 30
Maesbury Marsh *Shrp* 2B 30
Maes-hafn *Den* 1A 18
Magna Park *Leics* 3C 49
Maidenwell *Linc* 3B 16
Maidford *Nptn* 3C 61
Maids Moreton *Buck* 2D 69
Maidwell *Nptn* 1D 61
Mainstone *Shrp* 3B 42
Maisemore *Glos* 3C 65
Major's Green *Worc* 1B 58
Makeney *Derbs* 3D 23
Malcoff *Derbs* 2A 10
Malinslee *Telf* 1B 44
Malpas *Ches W* 3C 19
Malpas *Newp* 3A 70
Malswick *Glos* 3B 64
Maltby *S Yor* 1B 12
Maltby le Marsh *Linc* 2C 17
Malvern Link *Worc* 1B 64
Malvern Wells *Worc* 1B 64
Mamble *Worc* 1A 56
Mamhilad *Mon* 2A 70
Manafon *Powy* 1A 42
Manby *Linc* 2B 16
Mancetter *Warw* 2A 48
Mancot *Flin* 1B 18
Manea *Cambs* 3D 53
Maney *W Mid* 2C 47
Mansell Gamage *Here* 1B 62
Mansell Lacy *Here* 1C 63
Mansfield *Notts* 1B 24
Mansfield Woodhouse *Notts* 1B 24
Manthorpe *Linc* 3C 39
(nr Bourne)
Manthorpe *Linc* 1B 38
(nr Grantham)
Manton *N Lin* 3C 7
Manton *Notts* 3B 12
Manton *Rut* 1B 50
Maplebeck *Notts* 1D 25
Mapleton *Derbs* 3B 22
Mapperley *Derbs* 3A 24
Mapperley *Nott* 3B 24
Mapperley Park *Nott* 3B 24
Mappleborough Green *Warw* 2A 58
Mapplewell *S Yor* 3A 4
Marbury *Ches E* 3D 19
March *Cambs* 2D 53
Marcham *Oxon* 3D 75
Marchamley *Shrp* 2D 31
Marchington *Staf* 1B 34
Marchington Woodlands *Staf* 2B 34
Marchwiel *Wrex* 3B 18
Marden *Here* 1D 63
Mardu *Shrp* 3B 42
Mardy *Mon* 1A 70
Marefield *Leics* 1A 50
Mareham le Fen *Linc* 1A 28
Mareham on the Hill *Linc* 1A 28
Marehay *Derbs* 3A 24
Marfleet *Hull* 1A 8
Marford *Wrex* 2B 18
Marholm *Pet* 1A 52
Markby *Linc* 3C 17
Markeaton *Derb* 1D 35
Market Bosworth *Leics* 1B 48
Market Deeping *Linc* 3D 39
Market Drayton *Shrp* 1A 32
Market End *Warw* 3A 48
Market Harborough *Leics* 3A 50
Market Overton *Rut* 3A 38
Market Rasen *Linc* 2D 15
Market Stainton *Linc* 2A 16
Markfield *Leics* 3A 36
Marlcliff *Warw* 3A 58
Marley Green *Ches E* 3D 19
Marlow *Here* 1B 54
Marlpool *Derbs* 3A 24
Marr *S Yor* 3C 5
Marsh, The *Powy* 2C 43
Marsh, The *Shrp* 2A 32
Marshbrook *Shrp* 3D 43
Marshchapel *Linc* 1B 16
Marsh Gibbon *Buck* 3C 69
Marsh Green *Staf* 2C 21
Marsh Green *Telf* 3A 32
Marsh Lane *Derbs* 3A 12
Marston *Here* 3B 54
Marston *Linc* 3A 26
Marston *Staf* 2D 33
(nr Stafford)
Marston *Staf* 3C 33
(nr Wheaton Aston)
Marston *Warw* 2D 47
Marston Doles *Warw* 3A 60
Marston Green *W Mid* 3C 47
Marston Hill *Glos* 3A 74
Marston Jabbett *Warw* 3A 48
Marston Meysey *Wilts* 3A 74
Marston Montgomery *Derbs* 1B 34
Marston on Dove *Derbs* 2C 35
Marston St Lawrence *Nptn* 1B 68
Marston Stannett *Here* 3D 55
Marston Trussell *Nptn* 3D 49
Marstow *Here* 1C 71
Martin *Linc* 1A 28
(nr Horncastle)
Martin *Linc* 2D 27
(nr Metheringham)
Martin Dales *Linc* 1D 27
Martin Hussingtree *Worc* 2C 57
Martin's Moss *Ches E* 1C 21
Martley *Worc* 2B 56
Marton *Ches E* 1C 21
Marton *Linc* 2A 14
Marton *Shrp* 2C 31
(nr Myddle)
Marton *Shrp* 1B 42
(nr Worthen)
Marton *Warw* 2A 60
Mastin Moor *Derbs* 3A 12
Mathern *Mon* 3C 71
Mathon *Here* 1B 64
Matlock *Derbs* 2C 23
Matlock Bath *Derbs* 2C 23
Mattersey *Notts* 2C 13
Mattersey Thorpe *Notts* 2C 13
Maugersbury *Glos* 3B 66
Maund Bryan *Here* 3D 55
Mavesyn Ridware *Staf* 3A 34
Mavis Enderby *Linc* 1B 28
Maw Green *Ches E* 2B 20
Mawsley Village *Nptn* 1D 61
Mawthorpe *Linc* 3C 17
Maxey *Pet* 1A 52
Maxstoke *Warw* 3D 47
Mayfield *Staf* 3B 22
Maypole *Mon* 1B 70
Meadowbank *Ches W* 1A 20
Meadow Green *Here* 3B 56
Meadows *Nott* 1B 36
Meadowtown *Shrp* 1C 43
Meaford *Staf* 1C 33
Measham *Leics* 3D 35
Medbourne *Leics* 2A 50
Meden Vale *Notts* 1B 24
Medlam *Linc* 2B 28
Medlicott *Shrp* 2D 43
Meerbrook *Staf* 1D 21
Meer End *W Mid* 1C 59
Meers Bridge *Linc* 2C 17
Meeson *Telf* 2A 32
Meir *Stoke* 3D 21
Meir Heath *Staf* 3D 21
Melbourne *Derbs* 2D 35
Melton *E Yor* 1C 7
Melton Mowbray *Leics* 3D 37
Melton Ross *N Lin* 2D 7
Melverley *Shrp* 3B 30
Melverley Green *Shrp* 3B 30
Menithwood *Worc* 2B 56
Meole Brace *Shrp* 3C 31
Mepal *Cambs* 3D 53
Merbach *Here* 1B 62
Mercaston *Derbs* 3C 23
Mere Green *W Mid* 2C 47
Mere Green *Worc* 2D 57
Meretown *Staf* 2B 32
Meriden *W Mid* 3D 47
Merrington *Shrp* 2C 31
Merry Lees *Leics* 1B 48
Messingham *N Lin* 3B 6
Metheringham *Linc* 1C 27
Methley *W Yor* 1A 4
Methley Junction *W Yor* 1A 4
Mexborough *S Yor* 3B 4
Meysey Hampton *Glos* 3A 74
Michaelchurch *Here* 3D 63
Michaelchurch Escley *Here* 2B 62
Michaelchurch-on-Arrow *Powy* 3A 54
Micklebring *S Yor* 1B 12
Mickleover *Derb* 1D 35
Mickleton *Glos* 1B 66
Mickletown *W Yor* 1A 4
Mickle Trafford *Ches W* 1C 19
Middle Aston *Oxon* 3A 68
Middle Barton *Oxon* 3A 68
Middle Claydon *Buck* 3D 69
Middlecliffe *S Yor* 3B 4
Middle Duntisbourne *Glos* 2C 73
Middle Handley *Derbs* 3A 12
Middlehope *Shrp* 3D 43
Middle Littleton *Worc* 1A 66
Middle Maes-coed *Here* 2B 62
Middle Mayfield *Staf* 3B 22
Middle Rasen *Linc* 2C 15
Middle Street *Glos* 2A 72
Middleton *Derbs* 1B 22
(nr Bakewell)
Middleton *Derbs* 2C 23
(nr Wirksworth)
Middleton *Here* 2D 55
Middleton *Nptn* 3B 50
Middleton *Shrp* 1D 55
(nr Ludlow)
Middleton *Shrp* 2B 30
(nr Oswestry)
Middleton *Warw* 2C 47
Middleton Cheney *Nptn* 1B 68
Middleton Green *Staf* 1D 33
Middleton on the Hill *Here* 2D 55
Middleton Priors *Shrp* 2B 44
Middleton Scriven *Shrp* 3B 44
Middleton Stoney *Oxon* 3B 68
Middletown *Powy* 3B 30
Middle Tysoe *Warw* 1D 67
Middlewich *Ches E* 1B 20
Middlewood *S Yor* 1D 11
Middleyard *Glos* 2B 72
Midhopestones *S Yor* 1C 11
Midville *Linc* 2B 28
Milbury Heath *S Glo* 3D 71
Milcombe *Oxon* 2A 68
Milebrook *Powy* 1B 54
Miles Green *Staf* 2C 21
Miles Hope *Here* 2D 55
Milford *Derbs* 3D 23
Milford *Staf* 2D 33
Milkwall *Glos* 2C 71
Milldale *Staf* 2B 22
Mill End *Glos* 1A 74
(nr Northleach)
Millend *Glos* 3A 72
(nr Dursley)
Miller's Dale *Derbs* 3B 10
Millers Green *Derbs* 2C 23
Millfield *Pet* 1A 52
Mill Green *Shrp* 2A 32
Mill Green *Staf* 2A 34
Millhalf *Here* 1A 62
Millhouses *S Yor* 2D 11
Millington Green *Derbs* 3C 23
Millmeece *Staf* 1C 33
Millthorpe *Derbs* 3D 11
Millthorpe *Linc* 1D 39
Milltown *Derbs* 1D 23
Milnthorpe *W Yor* 2A 4
Milson *Shrp* 1A 56
Milthorpe *Nptn* 1B 68
Milton *Derbs* 2D 35
Milton *Notts* 3D 13
Milton *Oxon* 2A 68
(nr Bloxham)
Milton *Oxon* 3D 75
(nr Didcot)
Milton *Stoke* 2D 21
Milton End *Glos* 2A 74
Milton Green *Ches W* 2C 19
Milton Hill *Oxon* 3D 75
Milton Malsor *Nptn* 3D 61
Milton-under-Wychwood *Oxon* 1B 74
Milverton *Warw* 2D 59
Milwich *Staf* 1D 33
Minchinhampton *Glos* 2B 72
Minera *Wrex* 2A 18
Minety *Wilts* 3D 73
Miningsby *Linc* 1B 28
Minsterley *Shrp* 1C 43
Minster Lovell *Oxon* 1C 75
Minsterworth *Glos* 1A 72
Minting *Linc* 3D 15
Minton *Shrp* 2D 43
Minworth *W Mid* 2C 47
Miserden *Glos* 2C 73
Misson *Notts* 1C 13
Misterton *Leics* 3C 49
Misterton *Notts* 1D 13
Mitcheldean *Glos* 1D 71
Mitchel Troy *Mon* 1B 70
Mitcheltroy Common *Mon* 2B 70
Mitton *Staf* 3C 33
Mixbury *Oxon* 2C 69
Mixon *Staf* 2A 22
Mobberley *Staf* 3A 22
Moccas *Here* 1B 62
Moddershall *Staf* 1D 33
Moira *Leics* 3D 35
Mold *Flin* 1A 18
Mollington *Oxon* 1A 68
Monaughty *Powy* 2A 54
Monk Bretton *S Yor* 3A 4
Monk Fryston *N Yor* 1C 5
Monkhide *Here* 1A 64
Monkhopton *Shrp* 2B 44
Monkland *Here* 3C 55
Monks Kirby *Warw* 3B 48
Monkspath *W Mid* 1B 58
Monksthorpe *Linc* 1C 29
Monkswood *Mon* 2A 70
Monmarsh *Here* 1D 63
Monmouth *Mon* 1C 71
Monnington on Wye *Here* 1B 62
Montford *Shrp* 3C 31
Montford Bridge *Shrp* 3C 31
Montgomery *Powy* 2B 42
Monyash *Derbs* 1B 22
Moorby *Linc* 1A 28
Moorcot *Here* 3B 54
Moorend *Glos* 2A 72
(nr Dursley)
Moorend *Glos* 1B 72
(nr Gloucester)
Moorends *S Yor* 2D 5
Moorgate *S Yor* 1A 12
Moorgreen *Notts* 3A 24
Moorhaigh *Notts* 1B 24
Moorhall *Derbs* 3D 11
Moorhampton *Here* 1B 62
Moorhouse *Notts* 1D 25
Moorhouses *Linc* 2A 28
Moortown *Linc* 1C 15
Moortown *Telf* 3A 32
Morborne *Cambs* 2A 52
Morcott *Rut* 1C 51
Morda *Shrp* 2A 30
Mordiford *Here* 2D 63
More *Shrp* 2C 43
Moreton *Here* 2D 55
Moreton *Staf* 3B 32
Moreton Corbet *Shrp* 2D 31
Moreton-in-Marsh *Glos* 2C 67
Moreton Jeffries *Here* 1A 64
Moretonmill *Shrp* 2D 31
Moreton Morrell *Warw* 3D 59
Moreton on Lugg *Here* 1D 63
Moreton Pinkney *Nptn* 1B 68
Moreton Say *Shrp* 1A 32
Moreton Valence *Glos* 2A 72
Morley *Derbs* 3D 23
Morrey *Staf* 3B 34
Morridge Side *Staf* 2A 22
Morridge Top *Staf* 1A 22
Morthen *S Yor* 2A 12
Mortimer's Cross *Here* 2C 55
Mortomley *S Yor* 1D 11
Morton *Derbs* 1A 24
Morton *Linc* 2C 39
(nr Bourne)
Morton *Linc* 1A 14
(nr Gainsborough)
Morton *Linc* 1A 26
(nr Lincoln)
Morton *Notts* 2D 25
Morton *S Glo* 3D 71
Morton *Shrp* 2A 30
Morton Bagot *Warw* 2B 58
Morville *Shrp* 2B 44
Mosborough *S Yor* 2A 12
Mose *Shrp* 2C 45
Moseley *W Mid* 3B 46
(nr Birmingham)
Moseley *W Mid* 1A 46
(nr Wolverhampton)
Moseley *Worc* 3C 57
Moss *S Yor* 2C 5
Moss *Wrex* 2B 18
Mossgate *Staf* 1D 33
Mossley *Ches E* 1C 21
Moston *Shrp* 2D 31
Moston Green *Ches E* 1B 20
Moulton *Ches W* 1A 20
Moulton *Linc* 2B 40
Moulton *Nptn* 2D 61
Moulton Chapel *Linc* 3A 40
Moulton Eaugate *Linc* 3B 40
Moulton Seas End *Linc* 2B 40
Mounton *Mon* 3C 71
Mount Pleasant *Buck* 2C 69
Mount Pleasant *Ches E* 2C 21
Mount Pleasant *Derbs* 3D 23
(nr Derby)
Mount Pleasant *Derbs* 3C 35
(nr Swadlincote)
Mount Skippett *Oxon* 1C 75
Mountsorrel *Leics* 3B 36
Mow Cop *Ches E* 2C 21
Mowmacre Hill *Leic* 1C 49
Mowsley *Leics* 3D 49
Much Birch *Here* 2D 63
Much Cowarne *Here* 1A 64
Much Dewchurch *Here* 2C 63
Much Marcle *Here* 2A 64
Much Wenlock *Shrp* 1B 44
Mucklestone *Staf* 1B 32
Muckleton *Shrp* 2D 31
Muckley *Shrp* 2B 44
Muckley Corner *Staf* 1B 46
Muckton *Linc* 2B 16
Mugginton *Derbs* 3C 23
Muggintonlane End *Derbs* 3C 23
Mumby *Linc* 3D 17
Munderfield Row *Here* 3A 56
Munderfield Stocks *Here* 3A 56
Munsley *Here* 1A 64
Munslow *Shrp* 3A 44
Murcot *Worc* 1A 66
Murrow *Cambs* 1C 53
Muscott *Nptn* 2C 61
Muston *Leics* 1A 38
Mustow Green *Worc* 1C 57
Muxton *Telf* 3B 32
Myddle *Shrp* 2C 31
Mynydd-bach *Mon* 3B 70
Mynydd Isa *Flin* 1A 18
Mythe, The *Glos* 2C 65
Mytton *Shrp* 3C 31

N

Nailbridge *Glos* 1D 71
Nailstone *Leics* 1B 48
Nailsworth *Glos* 3B 72
Nanpantan *Leics* 3B 36
Nantmawr *Shrp* 2A 30
Nantwich *Ches E* 2A 20
Nant-y-Derry *Mon* 2A 70
Napton on the Hill *Warw* 2A 60
Narborough *Leics* 2C 49
Narth, The *Mon* 2C 71
Naseby *Nptn* 1C 61
Nash *Buck* 2D 69
Nash *Here* 2B 54
Nash *Shrp* 1A 56
Nassington *Nptn* 2D 51
Naunton *Glos* 3B 66
Naunton *Worc* 2C 65
Naunton Beauchamp *Worc* 3D 57
Navenby *Linc* 2B 26
Neal's Green *Warw* 3A 48
Needwood *Staf* 2B 34
Neen Savage *Shrp* 1A 56
Neen Sollars *Shrp* 1A 56
Neenton *Shrp* 3B 44
Neithrop *Oxon* 1A 68
Nelly Andrews Green *Powy* 1B 42
Nene Terrace *Linc* 1B 52
Nercwys *Flin* 1A 18
Nesscliffe *Shrp* 3B 30
Nether Broughton *Leics* 2C 37
Nethercote *Glos* 3B 66
Nethercote *Warw* 2B 60
Nethercott *Oxon* 3A 68
Nether End *Derbs* 3C 11
Netherend *Glos* 2C 71
Netherfield *Notts* 3C 25
Nether Handley *Derbs* 3A 12
Nether Haugh *S Yor* 1A 12
Nether Heage *Derbs* 2D 23
Nether Heyford *Nptn* 3C 61
Netherland Green *Staf* 1B 34
Nether Langwith *Notts* 3B 12
Nether Moor *Derbs* 1D 23
Nether Padley *Derbs* 3C 11
Netherseal *Derbs* 3C 35
Netherton *Here* 3D 63
Netherton *Shrp* 3C 45
Netherton *W Mid* 3A 46
Netherton *Worc* 1D 65
Nethertown *Staf* 3B 34
Nether Westcote *Glos* 3C 67
Nether Whitacre *Warw* 2D 47
Nether Worton *Oxon* 2A 68
Netley *Shrp* 1D 43
Nettleham *Linc* 3C 15
Nettleton *Linc* 3A 8
Newark *Pet* 1B 52
Newark-on-Trent *Notts* 2D 25
New Arley *Warw* 3D 47
New Balderton *Notts* 2A 26
New Barnetby *N Lin* 2D 7
Newbold *Derbs* 3D 11
Newbold *Leics* 3A 36
Newbold on Avon *Warw* 1A 60
Newbold on Stour *Warw* 1C 67
Newbold Pacey *Warw* 3C 59
Newbold Verdon *Leics* 1B 48
New Bolingbroke *Linc* 2B 28
Newborough *Pet* 1B 52
Newborough *Staf* 2B 34
Newbottle *Nptn* 2B 68
New Boultham *Linc* 3B 14
Newbridge *Wrex* 3A 18
Newbridge Green *Worc* 2C 65
Newbridge on Usk *Mon* 3A 70
New Brighton *Flin* 1A 18
New Brinsley *Notts* 2A 24
New Broughton *Wrex* 2B 18
Newcastle *Mon* 1B 70
Newcastle *Shrp* 3B 42
Newcastle-under-Lyme *Staf* 3C 21
Newchapel *Staf* 2C 21
Newchurch *Here* 3B 54
Newchurch *Mon* 3B 70
Newchurch *Powy* 3A 54
Newchurch *Staf* 2B 34
New Crofton *W Yor* 2A 4
New Duston *Nptn* 2D 61
New Edlington *S Yor* 1B 12
New End *Warw* 2B 58
New End *Worc* 3A 58
New England *Pet* 1A 52
Newent *Glos* 3B 64
New Fryston *W Yor* 1B 4
Newhall *Ches E* 3A 20
Newhall *Derbs* 2C 35
Newhaven *Derbs* 1B 22
New Holland *N Lin* 1D 7
New Houghton *Derbs* 1B 24
Newington *Notts* 1C 13
Newington Bagpath *Glos* 3B 72
New Inn *Mon* 2B 70
New Inn *Torf* 3A 70
New Invention *Shrp* 1A 54
Newland *Glos* 2C 71
Newland *N Yor* 1D 5
Newland *Worc* 1B 64
Newlands *Staf* 2A 34
New Leake *Linc* 2C 29
New Lenton *Nott* 1B 36
New Marton *Shrp* 1B 30
Newmillerdam *W Yor* 2A 4
New Mills *Derbs* 2A 10
New Mills *Mon* 2C 71
Newnham *Glos* 1D 71
Newnham *Nptn* 3B 60
Newnham *Warw* 2B 58
Newnham Bridge *Worc* 2A 56
New Ollerton *Notts* 1C 25
New Oscott *W Mid* 2B 46
Newport *Glos* 3D 71
Newport *Telf* 3B 32
New Radnor *Powy* 2A 54
New Rossington *S Yor* 1C 13
Newsbank *Ches E* 1C 21
New Sharlston *W Yor* 1A 4
Newsholme *E Yor* 1A 6
Newstead *Notts* 2B 24
New Street *Here* 3B 54
Newstreet Lane *Shrp* 1A 32
New Swannington *Leics* 3A 36
Newthorpe *Notts* 3A 24
Newton *Cambs* 3C 41
Newton *Ches W* 1C 19
(nr Chester)
Newton *Ches W* 2D 19
(nr Tattenhall)
Newton *Derbs* 2A 24
Newton *Here* 2B 62
(nr Ewyas Harold)
Newton *Here* 3D 55
(nr Leominster)
Newton *Linc* 1C 39
Newton *Notts* 3C 25
Newton *Nptn* 3B 50
Newton *Shrp* 2C 45
(nr Bridgnorth)
Newton *Shrp* 1C 31
(nr Wem)
Newton *Staf* 2A 34
Newton *Warw* 1B 60
Newton Burgoland *Leics* 1A 48
Newton by Toft *Linc* 2C 15
Newton Green *Mon* 3C 71
Newton Harcourt *Leics* 2D 49
Newton Hill *W Yor* 1A 4
Newton on the Hill *Shrp* 2C 31
Newton on Trent *Linc* 3A 14
Newton Purcell *Oxon* 2C 69
Newton Regis *Warw* 1D 47
Newton Solney *Derbs* 2C 35
New Town *W Yor* 1B 4
Newtown *Glos* 2D 71
(nr Lydney)
Newtown *Glos* 2D 65
(nr Tewkesbury)
Newtown *Here* 2D 63
(nr Little Dewchurch)
Newtown *Here* 1A 64
(nr Stretton Grandison)
Newtown *Powy* 2A 42
Newtown *Shrp* 1C 31
Newtown *Staf* 1D 21
(nr Biddulph)
Newtown *Staf* 1A 46
(nr Cannock)
Newtown *Staf* 1A 22
(nr Longnor)
Newtown Linford *Leics* 1C 49
Newtown Unthank *Leics* 1B 48
New Village *S Yor* 3C 5
New Walsoken *Cambs* 1D 53
New Waltham *NE Lin* 3B 8
New World *Cambs* 2C 53
New Yatt *Oxon* 1C 75
New York *Linc* 2A 28
Nextend *Here* 3B 54
Nib Heath *Shrp* 3C 31
Nobold *Shrp* 3C 31
Nobottle *Nptn* 2C 61
Nocton *Linc* 1C 27
No Man's Heath *Ches W* 3D 19
No Man's Heath *Warw* 1D 47
Noneley *Shrp* 2C 31
Norbridge *Here* 1B 64
Norbury *Ches E* 3D 19
Norbury *Derbs* 3B 22
Norbury *Shrp* 2C 43
Norbury *Staf* 2B 32
Nordley *Shrp* 2B 44
Normanby *N Lin* 2B 6
Normanby-by-Spital *Linc* 2C 15
Normanby le Wold *Linc* 1D 15
Norman Cross *Cambs* 2A 52
Normanton *Derb* 1D 35
Normanton *Leics* 3A 26
Normanton *Notts* 2D 25
Normanton *W Yor* 1A 4
Normanton le Heath *Leics* 3D 35
Normanton-on-Cliffe *Linc* 3B 26
Normanton-on-Soar *Notts* 2B 36
Normanton-on-the-Wolds *Notts* 1C 37
Normanton on Trent *Notts* 1D 25
Norris Hill *Leics* 3D 35
Northampton *Nptn* 2D 61
North Anston *S Yor* 2B 12
North Aston *Oxon* 3A 68

Uckinghall – Wolstanton

U

inghall *Worc.* 2C 65
ington *Glos* 3D 65
ngton *Shrp* 1A 44
ngton *Linc* 1D 51
ngton *Shrp* 3D 31
rd *Pet* 1D 51
n *Warw* 2D 59
by *Linc* 3C 17
by *N Lin* 2A 8
by Skitter *N Lin* 2A 8
Glos 3A 72
nhall *Warw* 2B 58
sthorpe *Leics* 3C 49
y *S Yor* 2A 12
gswick *Here* 3D 55
erdale *Shrp* 3D 31
er Tofts *S Yor* 2D 11
erton *Shrp* 2B 44
erwood *Notts* 2A 24
tone *Derbs* 3D 11
tone Green *Derbs* 3D 11
ott *Here* 3B 54
ampton *Here* 2B 54
ampton *Worc* 2C 57
Hatherley *Glos* 3D 65
adon *Glos* 3B 64
er Affcot *Shrp* 3D 43
er Arley *Worc* 3C 45
er Astrop *Nptn* 2B 68
er Benefield *Nptn* 3C 51
er Bentley *Worc* 2D 57
er Boddington *Nptn* 3A 60
er Booth *Derbs* 2B 10
er Brailes *Warw* 1D 67
er Breinton *Here* 1C 63
er Broughton *Notts* 2C 37
er Catesby *Nptn* 3B 60
er Coberley *Glos* 1C 73
er Cound *Shrp* 1A 44
er Cudworth *S Yor* 3A 4
er Dinchope *Shrp* 3D 43
er Eastern Green
W Mid 3D 47
er Elkstone *Staf* 2A 22
er Ellastone *Staf* 3B 22
er End *Derbs* 3A 10
er Farmcote *Shrp* 2C 45
er Framilode *Glos* 1A 72
er Grove Common *Here* 3D 63
er Hackney *Derbs* 1C 23
er Hambleton *Rut* 1C 51
er Hardwick *Here* 3C 55
er Haugh *S Yor* 1A 12
er Hayton *Shrp* 3A 44
er Heath *Shrp* 3A 44
er Hengoed *Shrp* 1A 30
er Hergest *Here* 3A 54
er Heyford *Nptn* 3C 61
er Heyford *Oxon* 3A 68
er Hill *Here* 3C 55
er Howsell *Worc* 1B 64
er Hulme *Staf* 1A 22
er Inglesham *Swin* 3B 74
er Langwith *Derbs* 1B 24
er Leigh *Staf* 1A 34
er Longdon *Staf* 3A 34
er Longwood *Shrp* 1B 44
er Lydbrook *Glos* 1D 71
er Lye *Here* 2B 54
er Maes-coed *Here* 2B 62
er Midway *Derbs* 2C 35
er Millichope *Shrp* 3A 44
er Minety *Wilts* 3D 73
er Mitton *Worc* 1C 57
er Netchwood *Shrp* 2B 44
er Nobut *Staf* 1A 34
er Oddington *Glos* 3C 67
er Outwoods *Staf* 2C 35
er Padley *Derbs* 3C 11
er Quinton *Warw* 1B 66
er Rissington *Glos* 1B 74
er Rochford *Worc* 2A 56
er Sapey *Here* 2A 56
er Slaughter *Glos* 3B 66
er Soudley *Glos* 1D 71
er Stowe *Nptn* 3C 61
er Strensham *Worc* 2D 65
er Swell *Glos* 3B 66
er Tankersley *S Yor* 1D 11
er Tean *Staf* 1A 34
erthorpe *N Lin* 3A 6
er Town *Derbs* 2C 23
(nr Bonsall)
er Town *Derbs* 2C 23
(nr Hognaston)
er Town *Here* 1D 63
ertown *Derbs* 1D 23
er Tysoe *Warw* 1D 67
er Wardington *Oxon* 1A 68
er Weald *Mil* 2D 69
er Weedon *Nptn* 3C 61
er Whiston *S Yor* 2A 12
erwood *Derbs* 2C 23
er Wyche *Worc* 1B 64
ingham *Rut* 2B 50
ington *Shrp* 1B 44
on *Ches W* 1C 19
on *Leics* 2A 48
on *Linc* 2A 14
on *Notts* 3D 13
(nr Retford)
on *Notts* 2D 25
(nr Southwell)
on *Nptn* 2D 61
on *Pet* 1A 52
on *W Yor* 2B 4
on *Warw* 3B 58
on Bishop *Here* 3A 64
on Cressett *Shrp* 2B 44
on Crews *Here* 3A 64
on Heath *Ches W* 1C 19
on Magna *Shrp* 3D 31
on St Leonards *Glos* 1B 72
on Snodsbury *Worc* 3D 57
on upon Severn *Worc* 1C 65
on Warren *Worc* 2D 57
ood *Cambs* 3B 52
marsh *Here* 1D 63
Usk *Mon* 2A 70
Usselby *Linc* 1C 15
Utkinton *Ches W* 1D 19
Utterby *Linc* 1B 16
Uttoxeter *Staf* 1A 34

V

Vauld, The *Here* 1D 63
Vennington *Shrp* 1C 43
Venn's Green *Here* 1D 63
Vernolds Common *Shrp* 3D 43
Vigo *W Mid* 1B 46
Viney Hill *Glos* 2D 71
Vowchurch *Here* 2B 62

W

Wadborough *Worc* 1D 65
Waddingham *Linc* 1B 14
Waddington *Linc* 1B 26
Wadenhoe *Nptn* 3D 51
Wadshelf *Derbs* 3D 11
Wadsley *S Yor* 1D 11
Wadsley Bridge *S Yor* 1D 11
Wadworth *S Yor* 1B 12
Wainfleet All Saints *Linc* 2C 29
Wainfleet Bank *Linc* 2C 29
Wainfleet St Mary *Linc* 2C 29
Waithe *Linc* 3B 8
Wakefield *W Yor* 1A 4
Wakerley *Nptn* 2C 51
Walcot *Linc* 1C 39
Walcot *N Lin* 1B 6
Walcot *Telf* 3D 31
Walcote *Leics* 3C 49
Walcote *Warw* 3B 58
Walcott *Linc* 2D 27
Walden Stubbs *N Yor* 2C 5
Waldley *Derbs* 1B 34
Wales *S Yor* 2A 12
Walesby *Linc* 1D 15
Walesby *Notts* 3C 13
Walford *Here* 1B 54
(nr Leintwardine)
Walford *Here* 3D 63
(nr Ross-on-Wye)
Walford *Shrp* 2C 31
Walford *Staf* 1C 33
Walford Heath *Shrp* 3C 31
Walgherton *Ches E* 3A 20
Walkeringham *Notts* 1D 13
Walkerith *Linc* 1D 13
Walker's Green *Here* 1D 63
Walkley *S Yor* 2D 11
Wall *Staf* 1C 47
Wallbrook *W Mid* 2A 46
Wall Heath *W Mid* 3D 45
Wallsworth *Glos* 3C 65
Wall under Heywood *Shrp* 2A 44
Walmley *W Mid* 2C 47
Walpole Cross Keys *Norf* 3D 41
Walpole Gate *Norf* 3D 41
Walpole Highway *Norf* 3D 41
Walpole Marsh *Norf* 3C 41
Walpole St Andrew *Norf* 3D 41
Walpole St Peter *Norf* 3D 41
Walsall *W Mid* 2B 46
Walsall Wood *W Mid* 1B 46
Walsgrave on Sowe *W Mid* 3A 48
Walsoken *Norf* 3C 41
Walterstone *Here* 3B 62
Waltham *NE Lin* 3B 8
Waltham on the Wolds *Leics* 2A 38
Walton *Derbs* 1D 23
Walton *Leics* 3C 49
Walton *Pet* 1A 52
Walton *Powy* 3A 54
Walton *Staf* 2C 33
(nr Eccleshall)
Walton *Staf* 1C 33
(nr Stone)
Walton *Telf* 3D 31
Walton *W Yor* 2A 4
Walton *Warw* 3C 59
Walton Cardiff *Glos* 2D 65
Walton Highway *Norf* 3C 41
Walton-on-the-Hill *Staf* 2D 33
Walton on the Wolds *Leics* 3B 36
Walton-on-Trent *Derbs* 3C 35
Wanlip *Leics* 3B 36
Wansford *Pet* 2D 51
Wanswell *Glos* 2D 71
Wappenbury *Warw* 2D 59
Wappenham *Nptn* 1C 69
Warboys *Cambs* 3C 53
Ward End *W Mid* 3C 47
Wardington *Oxon* 1A 68
Wardle *Ches E* 2A 20
Wardley *Rut* 1B 50
Wardlow *Derbs* 3B 10
Wardy Hill *Cambs* 3D 53
Waresley *Worc* 2C 57
Wargate *Linc* 1A 40
Warkworth *Nptn* 1A 68
Warmfield *W Yor* 1A 4
Warmingham *Ches E* 1B 20
Warmington *Nptn* 2D 51
Warmington *Warw* 1A 68
Warmsworth *S Yor* 3C 5
Warndon *Worc* 3C 57
Warslow *Staf* 2A 22
Warsop *Notts* 1B 24
Warsop Vale *Notts* 1B 24
Wartnaby *Leics* 2D 37
Warton *Warw* 1D 47
Warwick *Warw* 2C 59
Wash *Derbs* 2A 10
Washerwall *Staf* 3D 21
Washingborough *Linc* 3C 15
Wasperton *Warw* 3C 59
Wasps Nest *Linc* 1C 27
Watchfield *Oxon* 3B 74
Waterfall *Staf* 2A 22
Water Fryston *W Yor* 1B 4
Waterhouses *Staf* 2A 22
Waterlane *Glos* 2C 73
Waterloo *Here* 1B 62
Waterloo *Shrp* 1C 31
Water Newton *Cambs* 2A 52
Water Orton *Warw* 2C 47
Water Stratford *Buck* 2C 69
Waters Upton *Telf* 3A 32
Watford *Nptn* 2C 61
Wath upon Dearne *S Yor* 3B 4
Wattlesborough Heath *Shrp* 3B 30
Wauldby *E Yor* 1C 7
Waun *Powy* 3A 30
Waun, Y *Wrex* 1A 30
Waun-fach *Powy* 3A 30
Waverton *Ches W* 1C 19
Waxholme *E Yor* 1C 9
Way Head *Cambs* 3D 53
Webheath *Worc* 2A 58
Webton *Here* 2C 63
Weddington *Warw* 2A 48
Wednesbury *W Mid* 2A 46
Wednesfield *W Mid* 1A 46
Weecar *Notts* 1A 26
Weedon Bec *Nptn* 3C 61
Weedon Lois *Nptn* 1C 69
Weeford *Staf* 1C 47
Weekley *Nptn* 3B 50
Weeping Cross *Staf* 2D 33
Weethley *Warw* 3A 58
Weeton *E Yor* 1C 9
Welbourn *Linc* 2B 26
Welby *Linc* 1B 38
Welches Dam *Cambs* 3D 53
Weldon *Nptn* 3C 51
Welford *Nptn* 3D 49
Welford-on-Avon *Warw* 3B 58
Welham *Leics* 2A 50
Welham *Notts* 2D 13
Well *Linc* 3C 17
Welland *Worc* 1B 64
Wellesbourne *Warw* 3C 59
Wellingore *Linc* 2B 26
Wellington *Here* 1C 63
Wellington *Telf* 3A 32
Wellington Heath *Here* 1B 64
Wellow *Notts* 1C 25
Wellsborough *Leics* 1A 48
Wells Green *Ches E* 2A 20
Welshampton *Shrp* 1C 31
Welsh End *Shrp* 1D 31
Welsh Frankton *Shrp* 1B 30
Welsh Newton *Here* 1B 70
Welsh Newton Common *Here* 1C 71
Welshpool *Powy* 1B 42
Welton *E Yor* 1C 7
Welton *Linc* 2C 15
Welton *Nptn* 2B 60
Welton Hill *Linc* 2C 15
Welton le Marsh *Linc* 1C 29
Welton le Wold *Linc* 2A 16
Welwick *E Yor* 1C 9
Wem *Shrp* 2D 31
Wensley *Derbs* 1C 23
Wentbridge *W Yor* 2B 4
Wentnor *Shrp* 2C 43
Wentworth *S Yor* 1D 11
Weobley *Here* 3C 55
Weobley Marsh *Here* 3C 55
Wergs *W Mid* 1D 45
Wern *Powy* 3A 30
(nr Guilsfield)
Wern *Powy* 2A 30
(nr Llanymynech)
Wernyrheolydd *Mon* 1A 70
Werrington *Pet* 1A 52
Werrington *Staf* 3D 21
Wessington *Derbs* 2D 23
West Ashby *Linc* 3A 16
West Barkwith *Linc* 2D 15
Westborough *Linc* 3A 26
West Bridgford *Notts* 1B 36
West Bromwich *W Mid* 2B 46
Westbrook *Here* 1A 62
Westbury *Buck* 2C 69
Westbury *Shrp* 1C 43
Westbury-on-Severn *Glos* 1A 72
West Butterwick *N Lin* 3B 6
Westby *Linc* 2B 38
West Carr *N Lin* 3A 6
Westcott Barton *Oxon* 3A 68
West Cowick *E Yor* 1D 5
West Deeping *Linc* 1A 52
West Drayton *Notts* 3D 13
West Ella *E Yor* 1D 7
West End *Cambs* 2D 53
West End *Linc* 3B 28
West Farndon *Nptn* 3B 60
West Felton *Shrp* 2B 30
Westgate *N Lin* 3A 6
West Haddlesey *N Yor* 1C 5
West Haddon *Nptn* 1C 61
West Hagley *Worc* 3A 46
West Hallam *Derbs* 3A 24
West Halton *N Lin* 1C 7
West Handley *Derbs* 3D 11
West Hanney *Oxon* 3D 75
West Hardwick *W Yor* 2B 4
Westhide *Here* 1D 63
Westhope *Here* 3C 55
Westhope *Shrp* 3D 43
Westhorp *Nptn* 3B 60
Westhorpe *Linc* 1A 40
Westhouses *Derbs* 2A 24
West Keal *Linc* 1B 28
West Leake *Notts* 2B 36
Westley *Shrp* 1C 43
West Malvern *Worc* 1B 64
Westmancote *Worc* 2D 65
West Markham *Notts* 3D 13
West Marsh *NE Lin* 3B 8
Weston *Ches E* 2B 20
Weston *Here* 3B 54
Weston *Linc* 2A 40
Weston *Notts* 1D 25
Weston *Nptn* 1B 68
Weston *Shrp* 2A 44
(nr Bridgnorth)
Weston *Shrp* 1B 54
(nr Knighton)
Weston *Shrp* 2D 31
(nr Wem)
Weston *Staf* 2D 33
Weston Beggard *Here* 1D 63
Weston by Welland *Nptn* 2A 50
Westoncommon *Shrp* 2C 31
Weston Coyney *Stoke* 3D 21
Weston Favell *Nptn* 2D 61
Weston Heath *Shrp* 3B 32
Weston Hills *Linc* 3A 40
Weston in Arden *Warw* 3A 48
Weston Jones *Staf* 2B 32
Weston Lullingfields *Shrp* 2C 31
Weston-on-Avon *Warw* 3B 58
Weston-on-Trent *Derbs* 2A 36
Weston Rhyn *Shrp* 1A 30
Weston-sub-Edge *Glos* 1B 66
Weston-under-Lizard *Staf* 3C 33
Weston under Penyard *Here* 3A 64
Weston under Wetherley *Warw* 2D 59
Weston Underwood *Derbs* 3C 23
West Rasen *Linc* 2C 15
West Ravendale *NE Lin* 1A 16
Westry *Cambs* 2C 53
West Stockwith *Notts* 1D 13
West Torrington *Linc* 2D 15
Westville *Notts* 3B 24
West Walton *Norf* 3C 41
Westwell *Oxon* 2B 74
West Willoughby *Linc* 3B 26
Westwood *Pet* 1A 52
Westwoodside *N Lin* 1D 13
Wetley Rocks *Staf* 3D 21
Wettenhall *Ches E* 1A 20
Wetton *Staf* 2B 22
Wetwood *Staf* 1B 32
Weythel *Powy* 3A 54
Whaddon *Glos* 1B 72
Whaley *Derbs* 3B 12
Whaley Bridge *Derbs* 2A 10
Whaley Thorns *Derbs* 3B 12
Whaplode *Linc* 2B 40
Whaplode Drove *Linc* 3B 40
Whaplode St Catherine *Linc* 2B 40
Wharncliffe Side *S Yor* 1C 11
Wharton *Ches W* 1A 20
Wharton *Here* 3D 55
Whatcote *Warw* 1D 67
Whateley *Warw* 2D 47
Whatmore *Shrp* 1A 56
Whatstandwell *Derbs* 2D 23
Whatton *Notts* 1D 37
Wheatcroft *Derbs* 2D 23
Wheathill *Shrp* 3B 44
Wheatley *S Yor* 3C 5
Wheatley Park *S Yor* 3C 5
Wheaton Aston *Staf* 3C 33
Wheatstone Park *Staf* 1D 45
Wheelock *Ches E* 2B 20
Wheelock Heath *Ches E* 2B 20
Whelford *Glos* 3A 74
Wheston *Derbs* 3B 10
Whetstone *Leics* 2C 49
Whichford *Warw* 2D 67
Whilton *Nptn* 2C 61
Whirlow *S Yor* 2D 11
Whisby *Linc* 1B 26
Whissendine *Rut* 3A 38
Whiston *S Yor* 1A 12
Whiston *Staf* 3A 22
(nr Cheadle)
Whiston *Staf* 3C 33
(nr Penkridge)
Whiston Cross *Shrp* 1C 45
Whiston Eaves *Staf* 3A 22
Whitacre Heath *Warw* 2D 47
Whitbourne *Here* 3B 56
Whitchurch *Buck* 3D 69
Whitchurch *Here* 1C 71
Whitchurch *Shrp* 3D 19
Whitcot *Shrp* 2C 43
Whitcott Keysett *Shrp* 3B 42
Whitebrook *Mon* 2C 71
Whitecroft *Glos* 2D 71
White End *Worc* 2B 64
Whitegate *Ches W* 1A 20
Whitehaven *Shrp* 2A 30
Whitehough *Derbs* 2A 10
White Ladies Aston *Worc* 3D 57
Whiteoak Green *Oxon* 1C 75
White Pit *Linc* 3B 16
White Rocks *Here* 3C 63
Whiteshill *Glos* 2B 72
White Stone *Here* 1D 63
Whiteway *Glos* 1C 73
Whitfield *Nptn* 2C 69
Whitfield *S Glo* 3D 71
Whitgift *E Yor* 1B 6
Whitgreave *Staf* 2C 33
Whitley *N Yor* 1C 5
Whitley Heath *Staf* 2C 33
Whitley Thorpe *N Yor* 1C 5
Whitlock's End *W Mid* 1B 58
Whitminster *Glos* 2A 72
Whitmore *Staf* 3C 21
Whitnash *Warw* 2D 59
Whitney-on-Wye *Here* 1A 62
Whittingslow *Shrp* 3D 43
Whittington *Derbs* 3A 12
Whittington *Glos* 3A 66
Whittington *Shrp* 1B 30
Whittington *Staf* 3D 45
(nr Kinver)
Whittington *Staf* 1C 47
(nr Lichfield)
Whittington *Warw* 2D 47
Whittington *Worc* 3C 57
Whittington Barracks *Staf* 1C 47
Whittlebury *Nptn* 1C 69
Whittleford *Warw* 2A 48
Whittlesey *Cambs* 2B 52
Whitton *N Lin* 1C 7
Whitton *Powy* 2A 54
Whitton *Shrp* 1D 55
Whitwell *Derbs* 3B 12
Whitwell *Rut* 1C 51
Whitwick *Leics* 3A 36
Whitwood *W Yor* 1B 4
Whixall *Shrp* 1D 31
Whoberley *W Mid* 1D 59
Whyle *Here* 2D 55
Wibdon *Glos* 3C 71
Wibtoft *Warw* 3B 48
Wichenford *Worc* 2B 56
Wick *Worc* 1D 65
Wicken *Nptn* 2D 69
Wickenby *Linc* 2C 15
Wickersley *S Yor* 1A 12
Wickhamford *Worc* 1A 66
Widmerpool *Notts* 2C 37
Wiggenhall St Germans *Norf* 3D 41
Wiggenhall St Mary Magdalen *Norf* 3D 41
Wiggenhall St Mary the Virgin *Norf* 3D 41
Wigginton *Oxon* 2D 67
Wigginton *Staf* 1D 47
Wightwick *W Mid* 2D 45
Wigmore *Here* 2C 55
Wigsley *Notts* 3A 14
Wigsthorpe *Nptn* 3D 51
Wigston *Leics* 2D 49
Wigtoft *Linc* 1A 40
Wilbarston *Nptn* 3B 50
Wilcott *Shrp* 3B 30
Wildboarclough *Ches E* 1D 21
Wilden *Worc* 1C 57
Wildmoor *Worc* 1D 57
Wildsworth *Linc* 1A 14
Wildwood *Staf* 2D 33
Wilford *Nott* 1B 36
Wilkesley *Ches E* 3A 20
Wilksby *Linc* 1A 28
Willaston *Ches E* 2A 20
Willenhall *W Mid* 1D 59
(nr Coventry)
Willenhall *W Mid* 2A 46
(nr Wolverhampton)
Willersey *Glos* 2B 66
Willersley *Here* 1B 62
Willey *Shrp* 2B 44
Willey *Warw* 3B 48
Williamscot *Oxon* 1A 68
Willingham by Stow *Linc* 2A 14
Willington *Derbs* 2C 35
Willington *Warw* 2C 67
Willington Corner *Ches W* 1D 19
Willoughbridge *Staf* 3B 20
Willoughby *Linc* 3C 17
Willoughby *Warw* 2B 60
Willoughby-on-the-Wolds
Notts 2C 37
Willoughby Waterleys *Leics* 2C 49
Willoughton *Linc* 1B 14
Willow Green *Worc* 3B 56
Willslock *Staf* 1A 34
Wilmcote *Warw* 3B 58
Wilnecote *Staf* 1D 47
Wilsford *Linc* 3C 27
Wilson *Here* 3D 63
Wilson *Leics* 2A 36
Wilsthorpe *Linc* 3C 39
Wimblebury *Staf* 3A 34
Wimblington *Cambs* 2D 53
Wimboldsley *Ches W* 1A 20
Wimpstone *Warw* 1C 67
Winceby *Linc* 1B 28
Winchcombe *Glos* 3A 66
Wincle *Ches E* 1D 21
Winderton *Warw* 1D 67
Windley *Derbs* 3D 23
Windmill *Derbs* 3B 10
Windrush *Glos* 1A 74
Winestead *E Yor* 1C 9
Winforton *Here* 1A 62
Wing *Rut* 1B 50
Wingerworth *Derbs* 1D 23
Wingfield Park *Derbs* 2D 23
Winkburn *Notts* 2D 25
Winkhill *Staf* 2A 22
Winnal Common *Here* 2C 63
Winnington *Staf* 1B 32
Winnothdale *Staf* 3A 22
Winsford *Ches W* 1A 20
Winshill *Staf* 2C 35
Winslow *Buck* 3D 69
Winson *Glos* 2D 73
Winson Green *W Mid* 3B 46
Winster *Derbs* 1C 23
Winstone *Glos* 2C 73
Winteringham *N Lin* 1C 7
Winterley *Ches E* 2B 20
Wintersett *W Yor* 2A 4
Winterton *N Lin* 2C 7
Winthorpe *Linc* 1D 29
Winthorpe *Notts* 2A 26
Winwick *Cambs* 3A 52
Winwick *Nptn* 1C 61
Wirksworth *Derbs* 2C 23
Wirswall *Ches E* 3D 19
Wisbech *Cambs* 3C 41
Wisbech St Mary *Cambs* 1D 53
Wiseton *Notts* 2D 13
Wishaw *Warw* 2C 47
Wispington *Linc* 3A 16
Wistanstow *Shrp* 3D 43
Wistanswick *Shrp* 2A 32
Wistaston *Ches E* 2A 20
Wistow *Cambs* 3B 52
Witcham *Cambs* 3D 53
Witham on the Hill *Linc* 3C 39
Witham St Hughs *Linc* 1A 26
Withcall *Linc* 2A 16
Witherley *Leics* 2A 48
Withern *Linc* 2C 17
Withernsea *E Yor* 1C 9
Withington *Glos* 1D 73
Withington *Here* 1D 63
Withington *Shrp* 3D 31
Withington *Staf* 1A 34
Withington Marsh *Here* 1D 63
Withybrook *Warw* 3B 48
Witney *Oxon* 1C 75
Wittering *Pet* 1D 51
Witton *Worc* 2C 57
Wixford *Warw* 3A 58
Wixhill *Shrp* 2D 31
Wold Newton *NE Lin* 1A 16
Wolferlow *Here* 2A 56
Wolgarston *Staf* 3D 33
Wollaston *Shrp* 3B 30
Wollaston *W Mid* 3D 45
Wollaton *Nott* 3B 24
Wollerton *Shrp* 1A 32
Wollescote *W Mid* 3A 46
Wolseley Bridge *Staf* 2A 34
Wolstanton *Staf* 3C 21

Published by Geographers' A-Z Map Company Limited
An imprint of HarperCollins Publishers
Westerhill Road
Bishopbriggs
Glasgow
G64 2QT

HarperCollinsPublishers
Macken House, 39/40 Mayor Street Upper, Dublin 1, D01 C9W8, Ireland

www.az.co.uk
a-z.maps@harpercollins.co.uk

1st edition 2024

© Collins Bartholomew Ltd 2024

This product uses map data licenced from Ordnance Survey
© Crown copyright and database rights 2024 OS AC0000808974

AZ, A-Z and AtoZ are registered trademarks of Geographers' A-Z Map Company Limited

A catalogue record for this book is available from the British Library.

ISBN 978-0-00-865283-8

10 9 8 7 6 5 4 3 2 1

Printed in India

MIX
Paper | Supporting
responsible forestry
FSC
www.fsc.org
FSC™ C007454

This book contains FSC™ certified paper and other controlled
sources to ensure responsible forest management.

For more information visit: www.harpercollins.co.uk/green